D0479963

Preparing Your Campus for a Networked Future

Mark A. Luker, Editor

Foreword by Graham B. Spanier

Preparing Your Campus for a Networked Future

EDUCAUSE

Leadership Strategies No. 1

Jossey-Bass Publishers
San Francisco

Copyright © 2000 by Jossey-Bass Inc., Publishers, 350 Sansome Street, San Francisco, California 94104.

All rights reserved. No part of this publication may be reproduced, stored in a retrieval system, or transmitted, in any form or by any means, electronic, mechanical, photocopying, recording, or otherwise, without the prior written permission of the publisher.

This book is part of the Jossey-Bass Higher and Adult Education Series.

Jossey-Bass books and products are available through most bookstores. To contact Jossey-Bass directly, call (888) 378–2537, fax to (800) 605–2665, or visit our website at www.josseybass.com.

Substantial discounts on bulk quantities of Jossey-Bass books are available to corporations, professional associations, and other organizations. For details and discount information, contact the special sales department at Jossey-Bass.

 Manufactured in the United States of America on Lyons Falls Turin Book. This paper is acid-free and 100 percent totally chlorine-free.

Library of Congress Cataloging-in-Publication Data

Preparing your campus for a networked future / Mark A. Luker, editor; foreword by Graham B. Spanier.—1st ed.
        p. cm.—(EDUCAUSE leadership strategies series; no. 1)
Includes bibliographical references and index.
    ISBN 0-7879-4734-2 (pbk.)
    1. Universities and colleges—Computer networks—United States.   2. Internet (Computer network) in education—United States.   I. Luker, Mark A., 1947–
II. EDUCAUSE (Association).   III. Series.
    LB2395.7.P74   2000
    378'.0025'678—dc21   99-048099

FIRST EDITION
PB Printing   10 9 8 7 6 5 4 3 2 1

The EDUCAUSE Leadership Strategies series addresses critical themes related to information technology that will shape higher education in the years to come. The series is intended to make a significant contribution to the knowledge academic leaders can draw upon to chart a course for their institutions into a technology-based future. Books in the series offer practical advice and guidelines to help campus leaders develop action plans to further that end. The series is developed by EDUCAUSE and published by Jossey-Bass Publishers. The sponsorship of PricewaterhouseCoopers LLP makes it possible for EDUCAUSE to distribute complimentary copies of books in the series to more than 1,700 EDUCAUSE member institutions, organizations, and corporations.

EDUCAUSE

EDUCAUSE is an international nonprofit association with offices in Boulder, Colorado, and Washington, D.C. The association is dedicated to helping shape and enable transformational change in higher education through the introduction, use, and management of information resources and technologies in teaching, learning, scholarship, research, and institutional management. EDUCAUSE activities include an educational program of conferences, workshops, seminars, and institutes; a variety of print and on-line publications; strategic/policy initiatives such as the National Learning Infrastructure Initiative and the Net@EDU program; a research and development program; and extensive Web-based information services.

EDUCAUSE
- provides professional development opportunities for those involved with planning for, managing, and using information technologies in colleges and universities
- seeks to influence policy by working with leaders in the education, corporate, and government sectors who have a stake in the transformation of higher education through information technologies
- enables the transfer of leading-edge approaches to information technology management and use that are developed and shared through EDUCAUSE policy and strategy initiatives
- provides a forum for dialogue between information resources professionals and campus leaders at all levels
- keeps members informed about information technology innovations, strategies, and practices that may affect their campuses, identifying and researching the most pressing issues

Current EDUCAUSE membership includes more than 1,600 campuses and 150 corporations. For up-to-date information about EDUCAUSE programs, initiatives, and services, visit the association's Web site at http://www.educause.edu/, send e-mail to info@educause.edu, or call 303–449–4430.

PRICEWATERHOUSE COOPERS

PricewaterhouseCoopers is a leading provider of professional services to institutions of higher education, serving a full range of educational institutions—from small colleges to large public and private universities to educational companies.

PricewaterhouseCoopers (www.pwcglobal.com) draws on the knowledge and skills of 155,000 people in 150 countries to help clients solve complex business problems and measurably enhance their ability to build value, manage risk, and improve performance.

PricewaterhouseCoopers refers to the U.S. firm of PricewaterhouseCoopers LLP and other members of the worldwide PricewaterhouseCoopers organization.

Contents

Foreword

As chair of the Commission for Information Technologies of the National Association of State Universities and Land-Grant Colleges and a board member of the University Corporation for Advanced Internet Development, I have been fortunate to have had a bird's-eye view of the vast enhancements information technology has been making across the spectrum of education activities, enabling our institutions to do things we could not even imagine in just the recent past. Yet I also see the irony in the fact that as our institutions strive to keep up with technological advancements, we have a tendency to exceed the capacities of the systems we currently have available.

Advanced network projects such as Internet2 are rapidly developing the ability to support the dramatically expanding flow of digital communications in higher education and are enabling new applications such as media integration, interactivity, and real-time collaboration. Although high-speed networking has been promoted by research universities to support data-intensive applications, new network services and applications will be transferred quickly to all levels of educational use and to the broader Internet community.

These developments will have a tremendous impact on classroom teaching and learning, distance education, library resources, scholarly communication, and institutional cooperation. Colleges and universities, large and small, can benefit from the enhanced capabilities that advanced networking offers.

There can be no doubt that the next generation of digital networks will transform higher education. Increased access, added flexibility, enhanced outreach, and more active and collaborative learning will be hallmarks of our future. No institution of higher education can afford to be left behind in taking advantage of advanced networking to integrate learning into the lives of those we serve.

GRAHAM B. SPANIER
President
The Pennsylvania State University

Preface

Computer networks, especially the Internet, have emerged as the hottest technology of the 1990s. The Internet, it is said, will completely transform the worlds of business, research, personal communications, entertainment, and, not least, education. The World Wide Web is rapidly shrinking the globe in ways not possible with telephones and airplanes and is changing our historical notions of what it means to work and learn together. Computer networks, along with personal computers and the specialized "information appliances" yet to come, are beginning to change the basic structures and operations of our educational institutions—even the meaning of the term *institution*.

Yet computer networks have been with us for several decades. Why the intense interest just now? Is this a fad? Will it fade away?

Several related factors have worked together to fuel this remarkable explosion of interest and investment in the Internet:

- Development of affordable personal computers that can handle the rich graphics, audio, video, and other media required for multimedia communication

- The recent invention of affordable ways to rapidly send and receive massive amounts of information—including voice and even video signals—through fiber-optic cables using a single, common method called the Internet protocol (IP)

- Rapid expansion of this network to reach more deeply into each community and ever farther around the world

- Development of huge stores of on-line information of all types that can be accessed at any time through the network

The Internet, in short, has reached a critical mass and is rapidly passing through the stages of technological development from scientific research to engineering development to commercial production to essential utility service. The Internet will soon overcome its present performance limitations to support a universal communications capability that was, until just now, the stuff of science fiction.

The accelerating technical development of the Internet is supporting an even more important social and economic change, the emergence of the knowledge society. In the knowledge society the key resource is human knowledge and the ability to access and use new types and ever larger stores of information at ever greater rates of speed and effectiveness. An economy based on knowledge and information has never before been possible. It presents a wealth of new opportunities, many not yet even imagined, but it also makes strong new demands, particularly in the area of educating and training our citizens for new and changing roles.

Major Opportunities and Big Choices for Higher Education

Nowhere will these opportunities and demands be felt more strongly than in higher education. The fact that our primary stock-in-trade is knowledge suggests that embracing the new tools of networked information technology should dramatically transform and improve our effectiveness as an industry. At the same time, however, we know that this can occur only after we make substantial changes to the design and operation of longtime structures and methods. In other words, we know we must transform higher education.

What are our options? Although the range of responses to advanced networking will be characteristically broad across the higher education industry, it is clear that the issue cannot be ignored. No one has proposed that our traditional classroom methods can be scaled up to meet the global demands of the knowledge society. No one imagines that growing demands for lifelong education can be met through residential instruction. No one has proposed that we turn our backs on the promise of improving the quality of education through richer learning environments that support more active learning and more styles and choices. A wide variety of institutions, from traditional colleges to brand-new "virtual campuses," are gearing up to meet the challenge. Although the final result is still far from clear, it is now imperative that the leaders of every institution of higher education begin to understand, plan for, and lead their institutions through the changes ahead.

About This Book

This first volume in the EDUCAUSE Leadership Strategies series is designed to help university and college presidents and other top leaders in higher education understand and prepare for the impact of advanced networking on their institutions. It focuses on high-level issues, not technical details. It shares the visions and ideas of noted experts on the opportunities and challenges to come and seeks to place them within the context of finding a vision and strategic plan for an institution of higher education. Finally, it provides specific tips and recommendations on how individual leaders can work to prepare their institutions to be ready and waiting to take advantage of the new opportunities afforded by advanced networking.

The book opens with a chapter I cowrote with Carole A. Barone, a recognized leader in university information technology, who now leads the EDUCAUSE National Learning Infrastructure Initiative. After providing a brief introduction to the basic notions and terminology of advanced networking, the chapter focuses on the impact of advanced networking on our core activity—educating students—and on the major opportunities and challenges that will confront each institution as a result.

In Chapter Two, Clifford A. Lynch, an innovative leader in electronic technologies for libraries at the University of California and now the executive director of the Coalition for Networked Information, describes how advanced networking is bringing about a true revolution in a major supporting arena of higher education, the academic library. The emerging networked, digital libraries will be able to provide access never before possible, but only after serious problems of ownership, organization, access, funding, and professional development have been tackled.

Chapter Three provides an overview of the leading development project for advanced networking in higher education today. Douglas E. Van Houweling, a seminal leader of national and university networking at the University of Michigan and at the NSFNET and now the driving force within the University Corporation for Advanced Internet Development, describes the Internet2 project and its goals, methods, and status. Should every campus participate? If not, how will the results of the Internet2 project reach the rest of higher education?

Each campus must think globally and prepare locally to take advantage of the eventual benefits of projects such as Internet2. In Chapter Four, Philip E. Long, a recognized national expert on strategies for the development of campus networks and related technologies, presents a set of basic principles and building blocks that can be used to organize and plan for network services on any campus. His advice is key to campus planning today, and leaders need

not wait to begin to follow his thoughtful and practical recommendations.

Getting into advanced networking can be a daunting task, but
it can be simplified dramatically by working with other institutions
in your region. Regional neighbors often collaborate for traditional
reasons anyway, so it makes sense to join forces in preparing for
advanced networking. In Chapter Five, Ron Hutchins, the leader
of a prominent regional center for networking in higher education,
explains how such organizations can help their member campuses
with professional development, planning, and coordination, as well
as costs, and can provide a bridge to advanced networking as
"gigaPoPs," that is, points where campus networks meet to share
advanced technologies.

The U.S. government played a central and historic role in
extending the original Internet to reach broadly throughout the
community of research and higher education. What is the proper
role of the government in extending similar capabilities for advanced
networking? In Chapter Six you will hear from two leading experts
in government programs for research networking—George O.
Strawn, director of advanced networking and infrastructure research
and deputy assistant director of computer and information sciences
and engineering at the National Science Foundation (NSF), and
David A. Staudt, former program officer at NSF and now an EDU-
CAUSE staff member leading an NSF-supported program to promote advanced networking to the broader higher education
community. Their chapter addresses how the federal government
might stimulate the development of advanced networking throughout higher education, strengthening our national capabilities for
research, education, and economic development on a permanent
basis.

In Chapter Seven, Ellen Earle Chaffee, the energetic president
of two small universities known for their powerful applications of
computers and networking, demonstrates how far a campus can go

with few of the resources and opportunities available on a major research campus and shows why there is no need for small institutions to wait to begin implementing an aggressive networking agenda.

The book closes with my summary of the major points made by the contributing authors and articulation of the steps that can be taken by campus leaders to prepare their institutions for these important developments. In the end, I conclude, the most critical role for these leaders will be to provide ongoing, active leadership amid the institutional changes that will be required to fully participate in the emerging knowledge society.

Washington, D.C.   MARK A. LUKER
August 1999   Vice President
                                                             EDUCAUSE

Acknowledgments

I would first like to thank the chapter authors, who so generously contributed their time and wisdom. Each is recognized as a leading thinker and "doer" in his or her area. Together they make a powerful and instructive group, indeed. I have greatly enjoyed working with them over the years on information technology developments in higher education. Our joint creation of this book was a particular pleasure.

Next I must thank EDUCAUSE and its president, Brian Hawkins, for their strong support of both the process of developing new ways to use information technology to improve higher education and the corresponding process of spreading the news, the methods, and the capabilities for these improvements throughout the community. Many of our most fundamental technical advances in recent years have revolved around developing the Internet and discovering how best to use it for higher education. This book is one part of a larger EDUCAUSE effort to help the entire higher education community adapt these new opportunities to its best advantage.

EDUCAUSE Leadership Strategies series editor Julia A. Rudy deserves special recognition and thanks for her extensive help in organizing this first volume of a new series, for her deadlines, and for her good judgment and critical eye as all the pieces came together. I could not have done it without her.

I would also like to thank PricewaterhouseCoopers, a longtime partner of EDUCAUSE, for their generous support in sponsoring the EDUCAUSE Leadership Strategies series. This sponsorship ensures the distribution of each volume to more than 1,700 EDUCAUSE representatives at member institutions, organizations, and corporations.

Finally, I wish to express my gratitude to my wife, Sue Rohan, for her cheerful encouragement and support of this endeavor and all of my others.

M. A. L.

The Authors

Mark A. Luker is vice president of EDUCAUSE, where he heads Net@EDU, a thought-leadership coalition of college and university chief information officers (CIOs) and state network directors who work to advance national networking for both research and education through joint projects and federal policy. He also leads the EDUCAUSE office of government relations and policy analysis in Washington, D.C., which works with partner associations to help shape the emerging policy and legal framework of the Internet, intellectual property, and other issues of importance to higher education. Prior to joining EDUCAUSE, Luker served for two years as program director for advanced networking at the National Science Foundation and the federal Next Generation Internet project. He concurrently worked on issues of reorganization for networked access to digital information and other services as CIO at the University of Wisconsin, Madison, for five years. Luker received his Ph.D. in mathematics from the University of California, Berkeley, and served as a faculty member and then a dean at the University of Minnesota, Duluth, before moving into information technology management.

Carole A. Barone is vice president of EDUCAUSE, where her responsibilities include focusing on the National Learning Infrastructure Initiative. Before joining EDUCAUSE in 1998, she was ciate vice chancellor for information technology at the University of California, Davis. Previously, she was vice president for information systems and computing at Syracuse University. She holds a master's degree and a Ph.D. from the Maxwell School of Citizenship and Public Affairs at Syracuse University. Barone currently is a member of the New Media Centers Board and recently served on the National Policy and Planning Council of the University Corporation for Advanced Internet Development. She also served on the boards of CAUSE and Educom prior to their consolidation to form EDUCAUSE. She is the 1995 recipient of the CAUSE *ELITE* Award for Exemplary Leadership and Information Technology Excellence. Barone has long been active in information technology in higher education at the national level. She speaks and writes extensively on the impact of information technology on organizations.

Ellen Earle Chaffee has served as president of two North Dakota institutions, Mayville State University and Valley City State University, since 1993 through a unique partnership that won the 1996 administrative leadership award from the American Association of University Administrators. The universities are among the first dozen in the nation to provide notebook computers to all students as a tool for major changes in teaching and learning. They have been featured in three national studies of instructional innovation, won two national awards, and received several highly competitive federal and foundation grants. Chaffee has written five books and many articles on strategic management, quality, and leadership. She was national president of the Association for Institutional Research and the Association for the Study of Higher Education and served nine years on the national accrediting board for pharmacy education. Chaffee is a member of the Education Provider Review Council of Western Governors University. Her previous positions were in student affairs, equal opportunity, research, and state system academic affairs. She holds a Ph.D. in higher education administration and policy analysis from Stanford University.

Ron Hutchins is the director of engineering in the Office of Information Technology at the Georgia Institute of Technology. He holds a bachelor's degree in mathematics and computer science from Georgia Southern College and a master's degree in information and computer science from the Georgia Institute of Technology. His current interests are production network management, educational collaboration technologies, high-speed large-scale network design and management, and mobile and nomadic computing. Nomadic computing and remote access are at the core of his current doctoral research. Since 1991, Hutchins has overseen operations and development of the Georgia Tech computer network, one of the largest academic campus networks in the Southeast. He is the primary technical architect of the FutureNet project, which is expanding the current infrastructure of the Georgia Tech campus and modeling future network technologies for the state of Georgia. As part of FutureNet, Hutchins is currently developing innovative collaborations with area schools and learning centers to use technology to enhance learning. Since early 1997 he has provided technical leadership on the Southern Crossroads (SoX) initiative, a regional implementation of the Internet2 project.

Philip E. Long is director of ITS Academic Computing at Yale University. He holds a bachelor's degree in psychology from Yale University. Long has worked in various technical and management positions in information technology at Yale for twenty-eight years, developing infrastructure and facilitating the use of technology in support of academic programs. He is active nationally in various professional groups, including eight years on the board of Bitnet in its early years as trustee, secretary, or vice president. Long is an active consultant, working on strategic planning with colleges, universities, and university systems. He presents regularly at regional and national conferences on academic technology, networking, and related topics.

Clifford A. Lynch has been the director of the Coalition for Networked Information (CNI) since July 1997. CNI, jointly sponsored by the Association of Research Libraries and EDUCAUSE, includes approximately two hundred member organizations concerned with the use of information technology and networked information to enhance scholarship and intellectual productivity. Prior to joining CNI, Lynch spent eighteen years at the University of California Office of the President, the last ten as director of library automation, where he managed the MELVYL information system and the intercampus internet for the university. Lynch, who holds a Ph.D. in computer science from the University of California, Berkeley, is an adjunct professor at Berkeley's School of Information Management and Systems. He is a past president of the American Society for Information Science and a fellow of the American Association for the Advancement of Science. Lynch currently serves on the Internet2 Applications Council and the National Research Council Committee on Intellectual Property in the Emerging Information Infrastructure.

David A. Staudt joined EDUCAUSE as director of networking outreach to focus on providing information to higher education institutions to assist in upgrading their campus and wide-area networking capabilities. Prior to joining EDUCAUSE, he spent twelve years at the National Science Foundation, where he served in the Connections to the Internet Program, which helped about two thousand higher education institutions connect to the Internet. Staudt holds an MBA from Northwestern University and a bachelor's degree in petroleum engineering from Stanford University. He is a frequent speaker and workshop presenter at national and regional conferences on campus and wide-area networking. He also has thirty years of experience in data processing and networking positions within the federal government.

George O. Strawn is the director of the Division of Advanced Networking Infrastructure and Research at the National Science Foundation (NSF). He is on leave from Iowa State University, where he serves as director of the ISU Computation Center. Strawn served as NSFNET program director from 1991 to 1993 and continued in a quarter-time capacity at NSF, where he was involved with deploying the new Internet architecture. Strawn has been a member of the ISU Computation Center staff and a faculty member of the ISU Department of Computer Science for more than thirty years, serving as chair of the department from 1983 to 1986. He has also held several positions in the computer industry and has consulted for both business and government in areas of information technology. Strawn holds a Ph.D. in mathematics from Iowa State and a bachelor's degree from Cornell College.

Douglas E. Van Houweling is president and CEO of the University Corporation for Advanced Internet Development (UCAID). UCAID is a consortium of U.S. research universities which, in collaboration with private and public sector partners, is currently engaged in the Internet2 project to advance networking technology and applications for the research education community. Van Houweling is currently on leave from his post at the University of Michigan as a professor in the School of Information. Prior to undertaking his responsibilities at UCAID, Van Houweling was the dean for academic outreach and vice provost for information and technology at the University of Michigan. As dean, he was responsible for providing access to the university's learning environment, research activities, and service programs unconstrained by space and time. As vice provost, he was responsible for the university's strategic direction in the information technology arena. Van Houweling also holds academic appointments in the University of Michigan Business School and in the College of Literature, Science and the Arts, in the Department of Political Science.

Preparing Your Campus for
a Networked Future

1

The Role of Advanced Networks in the Education of the Future

Carole A. Barone, Mark A. Luker

Many have predicted that a global network of affordable multimedia computers, on-line libraries, student-centered "learningware," and enhanced human communications in general will improve access to high-quality education on a scale that simply cannot be accomplished today. Although this may be a compelling vision of the future, many details, methods, capabilities, and even principles necessary to achieve it are not yet clear. Recent rapid progress on several fronts, however, suggests that much of this vision can be realized—and sooner rather than later. There is an exciting ferment in the entire field, both within and outside traditional institutions of higher education.

This chapter first looks at how the emergence of an advanced Internet will break the access, performance, and cost barriers that in the past have presented an insurmountable obstacle to the new vision of education. It then discusses the more fundamental opportunities and challenges concerning missions, goals, roles, methods, organization, and evaluation that will face our institutions of higher education once the technical barriers have been removed.

1

Role of an Advanced Internet in High-Quality Education

Most discussions about new models for distributed learning assume that there will be an underlying network—which we will call the advanced Internet—that can support the rich variety of communications and interaction required at any location, at an affordable cost. Why should we believe this now, when no past efforts have satisfied all of these requirements? And just what are the requirements, anyway? The following discussion explores the underlying technologies required to support distributed learning and looks at basic performance requirements, past and future methods of delivery, and important cost factors. It shows how the advanced Internet will be the first affordable system that can meet all of the basic access requirements of the new learning model, both on campus and off, and how some of these developments will be driven and partially funded by a massive convergence of three global communications technologies into one.

Network Requirements for Distributed Learning

A glance at the Web today shows that we do not really have to wait for the advanced Internet to begin to participate in networked distance learning. This is because traditional lectures, presentations, demonstrations, and examples, which are mostly one-way communications to the student, represent a large fraction of a typical course. A standard classroom lecture can be delivered effectively as a video clip, in just the way we can watch a news report over the Internet or on television today. (Indeed, one-way television has been the primary mode of distance education.) Simply dividing a lecture into small segments that can be repeated, skipped, called up as needed, and used anytime (as on videotape) adds valuable flexibility. Links to high-quality multimedia examples further improve the presentation, as can the preparation and delivery of really outstanding content. In short, many of today's classroom experiences can be replicated using a network that supports sending video segments to any location one way, including today's Internet. Although the Internet will become the most cost-effective way to deliver this type of content for learning, the real power of the new technology lies well beyond mimicking television.

What about the human interaction that takes place in courses, when students ask questions, get help, work together, and discuss common problems? All of these activities take place on today's Internet as well, but with a distinct bow to the limitations of the network. All have been implemented successfully using e-mail, with special software called *groupware* that keeps track of who is in what group, organizes their threads of discussion, and shares relevant information with group members. This type of communication is called *asynchronous communication*, because it does not require that members of a group be on the network at the same time. Although the idea of saving messages to be read later may at first sound awkward, it is a real advantage for distributed learning, since learners' schedules often conflict. (Of course, asynchronous access is also one of the main benefits of voice mail and e-mail.) Alternate versions of groupware support *synchronous communication*, which allows the members of a group to "chat" over the network, instantly receiving and responding to messages from one another. Often called *chat rooms*, these arrangements are a low-speed and inexpensive electronic version of a small-group discussion. Both synchronous and asynchronous communications over networks have been used very successfully for instructors' office hours, group projects, study sessions, and other types of interactions essential to many courses.

What can the advanced Internet add to this picture? Well, it can add an actual picture, as well as voices. With an advanced network both synchronous and asynchronous communications can include natural voice and video so that all participants can see and hear one another. This format makes for communication that is not only easier than typing and reading but also richer, conveying the subtleties of expression and tone that are lost in textual communication.

Two-way video conferencing has proved to be very effective for business meetings and remote classrooms, but it has been too expensive for widespread use. Advanced networks will make this tool affordable for both classroom and "anytime, anywhere" education. Network-based curricula will support a full range of interaction, with students working alone with lectures, in study groups, and with tutors.

Related Critical Technologies

Campus-based courses depend heavily on readings, presentations, exhibits, examples, and other supporting information. These types of information are every bit as important in a distributed model, but using them in that setting depends to a much greater extent on affordable access to a high-quality collection that can be searched and retrieved through a network. Since almost all of the information in traditional libraries can be presented in digital form, these needs can be met, in principle, by digital libraries that augment the Web and improve on its structure and capability. Although successful on-line collections exist today for certain fields, there are substantial economic, intellectual property, licensing, authorization, preservation, and management barriers that must be overcome to achieve this goal in general. Organizations such as the Coalition for Networked Information and the Digital Library Federation are working actively on practical solutions to these problems. Meanwhile, there is a rapidly growing but less well organized collection of digital information for education on the Web, CD-ROMs, and other media, which can often satisfy specific objectives.

Perhaps the most important components of a distributed learning system will be modules of *learningware*—that is, special computer programs designed to help a student access and work with presentations, questions, experiments, and related information on specific topics. Learningware might support flexible access to text, photographs and charts, sound and video clips, and on-line data, all focused on some particular learning activity. Such digital content can be organized in many ways, however, to adapt to the particular background, learning styles, and scheduling needs of the learner. More important, the content can be *active*, requiring the learner to search, organize, reason, and experiment with the subject matter, perhaps using special tools, much as in a laboratory or seminar. This type of active learning is usually more effective than a passive lecture, whether or not one uses technology.

The Future Internet

The commercial promise of the Internet has led to intense pressures to improve performance and reduce costs. Thousands of signals can now be squeezed into the space that used to carry one. New and existing communications companies are crisscrossing the globe with comprehensive networks of fiber-optic cables costing billions of dollars. Satellite and radio companies are finding ways to provide Internet access to locations where there are no cables. Engineers are devising ways to send greater amounts of information using fewer bits of data. Electronic and optical devices continue to decrease in cost. The geographical distribution of information around the world is being shifted in response to demand for access. Network-aware applications especially tailored for educational requirements are under development in projects such as Internet2. All of these developments point to vast improvements in capacity and performance.

And what about cost? The cost to the consumer translates to price, which is as much a factor of supply, demand, and competition as of technology. It is most important to note that much of this new capacity introduces new competition between new providers who control alternate routes to the consumers. Prices for connections are beginning to drop in those markets that now support real competition. And the cost of network components will plummet at the same time that newer technologies come into mass production.

Why all this intense investment in the Internet? Precisely because the basic communications requirements for distributed learning overlap those for collaborative research, electronic commerce, access to government, personal and business communications, and even entertainment. Each of these activities could be served by an advanced Internet. This means that a solution to the high-quality, low-cost, "anytime, anyplace" Internet is worth billions of dollars. Such technology is now the subject of intense research and development in universities, government, and the private sector. It is widely agreed that the resulting systems will support a convergence of separate voice, video, and data communications technologies into a single advanced Internet that can replace much of the redundant investment we presently make in all three of these areas. Future homes, offices, and classrooms equipped with telephone or cable television connections will automatically enjoy the advanced network capabilities required for distributed learning.

Taken together, these technical and economic developments point to the possibility of a dramatic increase in access to affordable, high-quality education. Can our institutions of higher education, or their emerging competitors, successfully adapt to the new opportunities in time to realize the vision?

New Opportunities and Challenges for Higher Education

Teaching and learning models of the future assume universal access to the network. Advanced networks appear to offer an educationally and economically viable solution to the pressing need for access to higher education for both the traditional eighteen-to-twenty-two-year-old cohort and for the exploding number of "knowledge workers" who will require access to lifelong learning. It is envisioned that improvements in access to instruction, as well as to its quality and affordability, will occur both on traditional residential campuses and in virtual learning settings. What contextual elements will change as advanced networks enable distributed learning?

Social and Cultural Issues

With the realization that the twenty-first century will bring with it a set of social issues related to education, the mission of higher education is expanding to provide access irrespective of life circumstances—for example, age, employment status, geography, culture, ethnicity, and family responsibilities. *Access* means a number of things, from physical access to course materials (provided via the Internet or a learning device) to intellectual access to the subject matter (provided by a neutral, nonjudgmental context, enabled by network-based learningware).

The classroom lecture and its concomitant social relationships have been dominant forms in universities for centuries. Advanced networks and information technology will enable the development of a new pedagogy that nurtures learning among those for whom the traditional classroom model is not a viable form of access or road to academic success. Tensions on campus run high as institutions of higher education face social and economic pressures that their cultural and value systems, embedded in traditional modes of instruction, do not accommodate.

Distributed Learning Environments

Virginia Polytechnic and State University's Math Emporium project is an elegant example of a felicitous match of advanced networking capability with an institutional need (and desire) to provide access. Faced with burgeoning enrollments and inadequate funding to accommodate students in the traditional classroom model, the university's mathematics department embarked on a courageous effort to transform its approach to entry-level mathematics courses. The Math Emporium, a five-hundred-workstation learning center located in a former department store building, provides an active learning environment for more than ten thousand students (Moore and Rossi, 1999).

Using network-based learning modules and diagnostic quizzes, students work at their own pace to master the material. Faculty fulfill their class contact obligations by spending time in the Math Emporium, mentoring students when they encounter difficulty with the material. Ongoing assessment of the learning that is taking place alerts faculty to subject matter areas where students are experiencing general difficulty, which then prompts them to schedule short tutorial sessions on those topics.

Blacksburg, Virginia, is one of a growing number of communities that offer high-end network access to their residents. Consequently, students are also able to access and work with learningware from their homes. Emerging capabilities in authentication and streaming video theoretically will let the Math Emporium make quizzes, "mini lectures," and tutorial help available over the network. It is interesting to speculate whether, over the long term, students will continue to visit the Math Emporium for social reasons or if they will build their learning communities solely on the network. Anecdotal evidence from other campuses indicates that students are moving toward the formation of electronic communities and have less psychological need for in-person contact.

Enterprise-wide transformational change, such as that taking place at Virginia Tech, requires more than advanced networking; this type of reconceptualization of the learning environment also calls for radical changes in institutional policy and funding allocations. The Virginia Tech initiative is as much a study of a courageous group of faculty members and administrators motivated to change the culture of student-faculty relationships as it is a study of the enabling power of advanced networks. This is an example of decisive, strategic action by an institution that understands its priorities.

Advanced networking also enables true distance learning to occur, by making students' geographical location irrelevant to access. The Western Governors University (www.wgu.edu) speaks to the economic importance a number of state governors place on providing lifelong access to education for the citizens of their states. The University of Arizona's Southwest Project (dizzy.library.arizona.edu/swp/welcome.html) is an example of the use of the Internet to make a large depository of information available to the community, including community colleges and K–12 schools. Both of these examples point to the importance and power of collaboration in realizing successful distance learning.

A milestone was passed in March 1999 when Jones International University, a for-profit distance education venture, was accredited by the North Central Association Commission on Institutions of Higher Education. Jones offers bachelor's and master's degrees in addition to its certificate programs (Mendels, 1999). There are countless other examples of noncredit, credit, vocational, and degree-granting programs that are being offered to students in a distance learning format.

Few would dispute that advanced networks can serve as catalysts for distributed learning opportunities. Many would argue, however, that their capability has outpaced the policy, culture, and infrastructure of U.S. higher education, thus creating a new set of tensions and barriers. It is these tensions and barriers that the National Learning Infrastructure Initiative strives to address.

The National Learning Infrastructure Initiative and the Instructional Management System

The National Learning Infrastructure Initiative (NLII), an EDU-CAUSE program (www.educause.edu/nlii), emerged from the conviction that information technology has the power to bring about systemic change in higher education by transforming teaching and learning. It was formed to address lags in policy, culture, support, and infrastructure that create barriers to transformational change through technology. NLII projects focus on enhancing institutional readiness for such change.

One such project, the Instructional Management System (IMS) (www.imsproject.org), was conceived to build a framework of specifications, standards, and definitions around which interoperable products could be developed. IMS-compliant products will soon enable faculty to execute efficient searches on the Internet for relevant courseware and let them quickly and easily create, obtain, and tailor course modules to suit their individual curricula, tastes, and modes of expression. The IMS holds much promise as the key element of a technical infrastructure required to move gracefully to modalities for teaching and learning that address the issues of quality, access, and affordability.

Table 1.1 shows typical course management activities, linked here with the specifications that will enable such activities to take place in an interoperable, network-based environment.

The roles of faculty members and students will change in this new learning environment, as will relationships between faculty, students, administrators, vendors, and publishers. Students will take more responsibility for their own learning programs and outcomes. Faculty "will become teaching and learning process designers and managers as well as content specialists" (Massy, 1998, p. 15).

New Roles and Relationships

Advanced networks also hold the power to alter the social and business relationships surrounding the educational enterprise. Students and faculty alike bring past experiences and assumptions about teaching to the virtual classroom. Swept out of their traditional roles, with the dynamic of their relationship changed, both feel insecure. Students wonder if faculty are really teaching them if most of their learning appears to take place independently, from learningware accessed via the network. Faculty question their values and, indeed, their value and identity as teachers when they move from the position of control in the classroom to serving as a helper of individuals and small groups of students, especially since their intervention in the learning process often comes only at the invitation of the student.

Table 1.1. IMS Specifications

Activity	Specification Type
Find it	Metadata
Get it	Packaging
Run it	Runtime services
Track it	Profiles
Discuss it	Collaboration
Integrate it	Enterprise

Source: Developed by the authors in collaboration with Steve Griffin, technical director of the IMS project.

The more fully engaged student, owing to the active learning facilitated by information technology, will bring new assumptions to the faculty-student relationship. Faculty development will take on a new priority. Campus support services will consist largely of teams of faculty members, professionals with formal training in curriculum design and development, and information technologists, collaborating in a partnership that respects and values the critical scrutiny, special insights, and expertise that each contributes to the effort. Our familiar business models will no longer apply as the roles of producer and consumer shift and evolve.

New Educational Products and Economic Models

Some institutions of higher education are more ready than others to address the implications of advanced networking for their future goals, priorities, and economic viability. The hype associated with distance education has led some higher education institutions to flounder in attempting to enter an ill-defined market without clear institutional goals or a viable business plan. The higher education community is just beginning to grapple with the policy and cultural barriers to successful entry into the distance learning economy. Some suggest that those barriers may not come down quickly enough to forestall massive structural change.

Lee Alley, former director of Global Market Development at KPMG Peat Marwick, provides convincing data of the impending explosion of demand for lifelong education. According to Alley (1999), the market population of demand for lifelong learning is currently over 165 million persons in the eighteen to sixty-four age group. This demand is coming both from individuals and from the industries that employ them. Alley implies that traditional institutions of higher education will be too slow to overcome the barriers to the type of transformational change required to address this demand. Wall Street cannot afford to ignore this huge market for lifelong education. Consequently, new corporate educational entities will rapidly emerge. E-commerce, in this context, becomes both *educational* and *electronic* commerce.

Alley paints a future higher education landscape that looks dramatically different from what we know today. In his scenario the role of some traditional campuses will change to a focus on providing a venue for campus life and socialization of the traditional eighteen-to- otwenty-two-year-old age cohort; others will find themselves among providers of core courses, whether to students on other campuses or in remote home and business locations. For-profit vendors will provide locally unique or specialty courses. Alley predicts that pricing for commodity (core) courses will contract to the lowest level available among a few branded institutions with high volume and low overhead, resulting in the following provider mix:

- 10 medallion brand institutions

- 100 dominant provider institutions

- 1,000 consortia collaborators

- 2,000 consumer institutions

- 10,000 for-profit vendors

If these projections are borne out, then we will see a rapid unbundling of campus-based student services from per-credit-hour pricing, new credit repositories and services, and the emergence of credit brokering and credentialing services. Advanced networks are again the enabling force behind these changes, because they allow students to be enrolled simultaneously with multiple educational providers, irrespective of their location. In addition to its work on an interoperable teaching and learning standards infrastructure, the IMS is geared toward the development of the standards and specifications to record and report the outcomes of the virtual classroom experience.

Summary

Advanced networks are on the cusp of new breakthroughs in communication capabilities. However, the tool is not going to be the solution unless we address its social, economic, and policy implications in concert with the expansion of advanced networks. Not all such technical capability will have a positive effect in addressing pressing social issues. To some these emerging capabilities (such as the ability to see and hear others communicating over a network) appear attractive because they will enable teaching and learning to occur in ways that are analogous to the traditional classroom. Although such capability may enhance some interactions, it may not be the technology of choice to neutralize certain types of biases found in the traditional classroom setting (such as cultural, ethnic, gender, or age biases).

Moreover, advanced networks will contribute to the advancement of those institutions of higher education that understand that their commitment to transformation must be grounded in realistic self-knowledge. Those who seek to enjoy the benefits of advanced networks need to match the capabilities of the technology to the aims of the institution.

Conclusion

Taken together, these developments in the technology and organization of teaching and learning and the emergence of powerful and affordable networks present a unique opportunity to dramatically improve access to affordable, high-quality education. Such improvements will be needed to help meet the greatly increased demand for all types of education, but they are certain to involve widespread, systemic changes in the way we organize these activities today. Since the issues we discuss involve and encompass the core mission of our campuses, they will rise to the awareness and concern of all the stakeholders in higher education. We are entering an era of fundamental change that will demand leadership as few eras have before.

References

Alley, L. "Cloning the Ivy Tower on Wall Street." Paper presented at the National Learning Infrastructure Initiative Conference, New Orleans, Feb. 1999. [www.educause.edu/nlii/meetings/orleans99/alley.html]

Massy, W. "Understanding New Faculty Roles and Work Patterns." In *Technology and Its Ramifications for Data Systems: Report of the Policy Panel on Technology*. NCES 98–279. Washington, D.C.: U.S. Department of Education, 1998.

Mendels, P. "Online Education Gets a Credibility Boost." *New York Times, Technology Cybertimes*, Mar. 13, 1999.

Moore, A. H., and Rossi, J. "Virginia Tech's Math Emporium: Curriculum Transformation Assessment in an Advanced Learning Center." Paper presented at the National Learning Infrastructure Initiative Conference, New Orleans, Feb. 1999. [math.vt.edu/people/rossi/mathemporium.ppt]

2

The Academic Library in the Networked Information Age

Clifford A. Lynch

Few ideas have so captured the public imagination as that of making all the world's knowledge available on the Net, of creating a comprehensive, organized, universally accessible virtual library that is free for all. It is a compelling vision, and it is particularly seductive for higher education executives besieged by demands for increased library budgets and new library buildings. Although the vision of the World Wide Web as a universal digital library is commonplace in the popular press (and indeed is becoming integrated into the expectations of some faculty and students), the reality is much more complex. Networked electronic information will not prove to be a panacea for institutions of higher education, although it does offer some tremendous opportunities. This chapter offers a concise, high-level briefing on the current state of electronic information and digital libraries and on the prospects for the academic library in the networked information age.

Digital Libraries and Digital Collections

The term *digital library* became popular during a large-scale research funding initiative by the National Science Foundation, the National Aeronautics and Space Administration, and the Advanced Research Projects Agency in the mid-1990s. This initiative built on two decades of investment in the development and deployment of the Internet. Although there is no universal agreement on the exact meaning of the term, a digital library is generally considered to be a coherent, comprehensive collection of electronic information and network-based services that support a specific user community, such as researchers in a given discipline. Some experimental digital libraries not only provide information but also offer tools for analysis and collaboration. Here they begin to overlap with other network-based systems, such as "collaboratories," which are virtual environments created to support research collaboration, control of remote scientific instrumentation, and data analysis. Many of the digital library efforts funded by the aforementioned initiative have dealt with nontextual material. One project focused on geospatial data (maps, photographs, and remote sensing data), and another concentrated on video information. Most digital libraries today are still research efforts, and there are serious questions about their sustainability as they move beyond the prototype stage.

A few commercial developments can plausibly be characterized as digital libraries, such as the legal databases offered by Lexis and Westlaw. These products provide comprehensive access to legal literature to practicing attorneys and law schools (under special discount programs), but their very high costs limit use by the broader academic community. In some disciplines (computer science and chemistry, for example), where scholarly societies control a substantial part of the key literature, these societies are now offering products they call digital libraries; however, I know of no single society that publishes enough of the literature in its discipline to provide a comprehensive disciplinary information resource. It appears that aggregating content from multiple publishers—as is done by Lexis and Westlaw—will be a central characteristic of digital libraries. As more commercial digital libraries become operational and economically viable, academic libraries may contract for access to such products on behalf of their users.

Although digital libraries remain largely a research enterprise, university libraries are increasingly including massive electronic information resources in their collections. These include licensed access to thousands of electronic scholarly journals and to databases that index the journal literature; scientific databanks, both public and commercial; licensed collections of cultural heritage images; and free access to a host of data files and documents provided by government agencies, research groups, and scholarly societies. Electronic information is claiming a growing proportion of the acquisitions budgets in research libraries. These electronic resources are tremendously popular with library patrons. Their convenience, timeliness, and accessibility beyond the library walls (by any authorized user) encourages more intensive use than do the printed materials they are supplanting.

The broader library community is now also moving rapidly to license electronic resources to support their institutional programs, largely through the vehicle of regional library consortia. Research libraries were the focus of most early efforts to license electronic information, although some public and college libraries were aggressive early adopters as well. It is now becoming possible, however, for a college library (as opposed to a research library) to think seriously about shifting much of its new journal and reference acquisitions to electronic form.

Due to the limitations of computer display technology, paper is still heavily used as a user interface for longer works, such as journal articles, which are typically printed on demand, article by article, for study by the user. Some formats, such as scholarly monographs, are still awkward in the digital environment, unless they are fundamentally redesigned. But experiments in these areas are moving forward. And many key reference books—such as dictionaries and encyclopedias—have already been successfully recast as computer databases.

Academic libraries crossed a crucial threshold once they decided that key parts of the information they provide would no longer be held locally (in printed form or on media such as CD-ROMs) but would be obtained by licensed access to network-based information services. This step beyond the traditional library function requires high-quality, reliable campus network connections for the delivery of library services that are relevant to almost every member of the campus community. And with every passing year, this community is more critically dependent on the network for its library services.

Yet the historical scholarly literature and our broader cultural heritage remain primarily in print form. Although the proportion of new contributions in electronic form grows year by year, research libraries already hold vast print collections. Converting these collections to electronic format is an enormous, costly undertaking, impeded by copyright issues as well as by the scope of capturing and organizing the materials in digital form. Comprehensive availability of the holdings of major research libraries in digital form is many years away. Important programs, such as the JSTOR initiative, funded by the Mellon Foundation, are digitizing comprehensive back runs of key scholarly journals. JSTOR, in particular, is significantly improving access to the historical literature at smaller institutions that may not have these materials in print form, by making them available digitally at affordable prices. Indeed, for smaller libraries, one can hope that within the next decade we may see retrospective files available that are nearly as comprehensive as existing print holdings. This will be a critical enabling factor in the development of high-quality distance education programs.

Although the comprehensive, systematic, retrospective conversion of the printed literature presents a huge long-term challenge, libraries, museums, and archives are enlarging their electronic collections in other ways. They are employing information technology to make the parts of their collections that are relatively unencumbered by copyright restrictions much more accessible and visible. They are converting special collections—manuscripts, photographs, paintings, maps, and other fragile, unique materials that traditionally have had to be carefully protected and minimally used—into digital representations that are available to the scholarly community worldwide. Researchers, faculty, and students everywhere can work with these unique materials, which were once accessible to only the privileged few who could physically visit them.

There are complex policy and economic issues here that are still largely unresolved. Museums, for example, gain revenue by licensing the reproduction of images of works in their collections and are still trying to resolve what they will give away and what they will charge for. University libraries with extensive, high-value special collections are facing similar dilemmas. Indeed, if unique collections become freely shared among the academic community worldwide, this raises questions about how superb research collections contribute to making a university great, and why a research university should continue to pay for them as their benefits become diffused across the broader community. In the future, the unique competitive contribution of a great research library may lie more in the overall breadth of information resources it makes available, the expertise of its staff, and the quality of its services than in its unique special collections. How widely these materials will be shared, and on what economic basis, remains open to question.

Virtually all conversion of special collections is based on imaging technology—taking digital pictures of physical artifacts. The resulting electronic files are large and, from a networking perspective, bandwidth-intensive. (By contrast, most "born digital" content is designed for efficient delivery in a networked environment.) The growing availability of these image materials will require continued investments in increased capacity, both for on-campus and wide-area networks.

As we gain more experience with commercially available electronic information resources, some of the technical attributes that seemed to offer so much potential are proving impossible to realize on a practical business basis. Electronic resources are licensed for specific user communities, and the license fees are tied to the size of those communities. Libraries cannot use electronic information resources to extend historic interlibrary loan arrangements into very-large-scale network-enabled collection sharing between institutions without paying for the increased use. This should not be surprising. Publishers naturally structure their offerings in the networked environment to preserve their accustomed revenue streams, and they have worked within the legal frameworks of copyright and contract law to accomplish this.

Electronic information will be an increasingly important part of the intellectual riches that libraries provide to the campus community. It is more flexible and more accessible than the print information it is replacing. But electronic information will not, by itself, resolve many of the problems involved in the information explosion and the uncontrolled growth of costs for scholarly information.

Electronic Information, Budgets, and Buildings

University libraries have been struggling with a major crisis in the explosive growth of scholarly publications—particularly journals—over the past two decades. Figure 2.1 shows pricing and acquisition trends charted by the Association of Research Libraries (ARL). The reasons for these devastating trends are complex and derive from fundamental structural problems in the system of scholarly communication that are beyond the scope of this chapter. For an introduction to these issues, see the Pew Higher Education Round Table's special issue of *Policy Perspectives*, "To Publish and Perish" (1998).

A few specific points about the relationship between the transition to electronic information resources and the budgetary problems facing libraries are highly pertinent here, and they are not good news. There is no evidence that a move to electronic formats will reduce the price of costly, low-circulation scholarly commercial journals. Most of the cost of such print journals is not in printing and shipping. There may be some relief around the margins. By joining consortia, small colleges and universities may gain access to extensive bodies of additional materials at a modest incremental cost; research universities may be able to add access to additional journals from the commercial publishers at low marginal cost if they

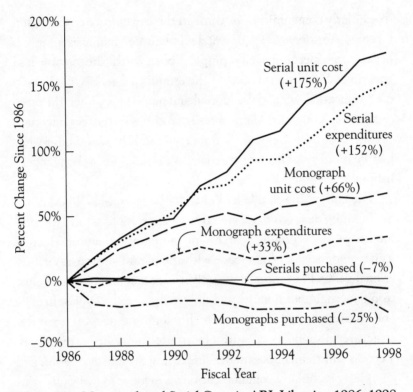

Figure 2.1. Monograph and Serial Costs in ARL Libraries, 1986–1998

Source: Association of Research Libraries, Statistics and Measurement Program, 1998. Copyright 1998 Association of Research Libraries.

maintain their large existing investments. But any actual reduction in expenditures will likely be tied to consortial bulk licensing agreements and multiyear contracts, and they will probably be modest. And for other types of materials—for example, an encyclopedia that's important for any academic library—costs for electronic versions will be much higher than the historic costs for print versions, although the electronic resources will be much richer, more accessible, and more heavily used than the books they replace.

In some sense, the networked environment does reduce barriers to scholarly publishing and allows an array of exciting enhancements to scholarly communications through the capabilities of the digital medium. A variety of experimental scholarly communications enterprises are emerging that compete both with the established commercial publishers and with the established genres of scholarly communication, such as the journal and monograph. Over the coming decade, competitive pressures from these initiatives may help control cost increases from commercial publishers and offer what may be more cost-effective alternatives to traditional scholarly publishing.

The end of this decade looks bad for budgets. Most libraries are maintaining dual print and electronic subscriptions while the community resolves long-term archiving of digital formats and faculty gain experience and confidence with the digital versions. A generational shift will eventually see universal reader acceptance of electronic journals, but libraries and universities need to invest heavily and continually in information technology and networking infrastructure to support access to electronic information resources. There is still tremendous inertia supporting the existing genres and channels of scholarly communication, as evidenced by faculty concerns regarding tenure and promotion reviews. Such conservatism will slow the development and adoption of new alternatives. College libraries with less comprehensive collections and less concern for archival responsibilities may actually be able to complete the transition more rapidly if they can afford the necessary investments in their information technology infrastructure.

New library buildings require capital funds, which are not typically considered part of the library's budget. As university administrators are well aware, continually funding new buildings to house annual collection growth measured in shelf-miles requires huge investments. But each year, money spent on electronic rather than print information is increasing. The need for additional collection space will probably decrease, and conversion of existing print holdings to electronic format will free up existing space. It is possible that within the next decade we will see library space demands approach a steady state—if faculty are willing to permit large-scale replacement of print collections by electronic information.

Although it may help contain costs for building new space, the growth of networked information will require funds to renovate existing space. Libraries will need to reconfigure space for new programs: they will want workstations for access to electronic resources, and they will need seminar rooms and teaching facilities in which to teach the university community to navigate and use digital information. Libraries will need facilities for scanning and digitizing special collections and space for faculty and students working on the design and creation of new multimedia works.

New Content and New Library Roles

I have discussed continuity and evolution, the gradual shift of library acquisitions from printed to electronic scholarly content, and the slow conversion of existing physical collections into digital form. But some of the most exciting possibilities offered by the developing advanced networks and the eventual widespread commercial deployment of these technologies are more revolutionary in nature: they take us to new genres and practices in scholarly communication and to new roles for libraries. Most of these effects will probably be felt first at research universities.

Advanced networks—starting with current Internet2 project developments—will powerfully change the way scholarly communication, research collaboration, and even teaching at the graduate level take place at the world's premier universities.

Internet2 will be a hospitable environment for the deployment of collaboratories—environments in which researchers in geographically scattered locations can cooperatively analyze data, control instrumentation, explore simulations, and author research. Even the collaboratory sessions can be captured as digital artifacts for review, annotation, distribution, and archiving. Libraries will play an important role in managing these collaboratories.

On a less technologically sophisticated level, the advanced Internet will allow groups of peer institutions to share seminars and advanced graduate classes. Both the diversity of the graduate educational experience and the informal early dissemination and vetting of new research will be enhanced by inexpensive video capture technologies and the ability of the advanced Internet to distribute video streams to remote classrooms and individual workstations. Such materials will need to be archived, annotated, retrieved, and redistributed, and libraries will become involved in organizing, indexing, and managing them.

Web sites by individual scholars or research groups are becoming important focal points for scholarship. Such sites combine aspects of databases, monographs, encyclopedias, and textbooks and can incorporate source materials and multimedia content (such as videos) that cannot be distributed using traditional media. Advanced networks will improve access to these sites with integral use of bandwidth-intensive multimedia. Because these sites exist outside the traditional framework of scholarly publishing, we need to institutionalize their maintenance, to ensure that their contents are archived and are continually available. Since research libraries have traditionally taken responsibility for archiving scholarly materials, they may play a role in archiving scholarly Web sites as well.

The extent to which these new genres will supplement or supplant existing vehicles of scholarly communication and publication remains an open question.

Finally, the efforts of EDUCAUSE's National Learning Infrastructure Initiative and the Instructional Management System project have placed us at the beginning of a revolution in the development of reusable, sharable, instructional media. The Internet2 environment will allow the distribution and sharing of more complex digital instructional materials for individualized instruction and distance education courses. The management of these materials at the institutional level and the mechanisms for sharing them across institutions will raise new questions about faculty and institutional rights to intellectual property, organizational roles, and responsibilities within the university for the stewardship of instructional assets. For example, current ideas about textbooks and course materials are likely to shift substantially; the digital analogue of a textbook may become much more tightly integrated with other course materials, and institutions might purchase (or issue) licenses for student use of the materials rather than have students purchase individual copies. The revolution in instructional media will likely move quickly beyond the research universities and may have its greatest near-term impact elsewhere in higher education. Electronic research and course materials will be used at all types of institutions, not just by a limited number of researchers and advanced graduate students. Indeed, economies of scale suggest that investments in developing electronic course materials will be made first for widely taught classes, such as large undergraduate lecture courses. Finally, although such materials can be transmitted from campus to campus, they will be used locally; thus a good campus network and computing infrastructure, rather than a fast and costly wide-area network connection, may be the key enabling technology for their deployment.

As advanced broadband networks built on technologies pioneered by Internet2 become commercially available and reach more educational institutions, libraries, businesses, and homes, the stage will be set for broader collaborations and sophisticated multimedia-based distance education. Libraries will increasingly work with faculty on rights management and licensing issues to support distance education by establishing virtual "reserve rooms," creating digital reference collections, and developing and managing instructional materials and documentation of research results. They will also work with faculty to help the university community—including distance learners—navigate and evaluate networked information resources and resolve issues related to authoring in this new environment.

With the passage of the Digital Millennium Copyright Act in 1998, the higher education community gained new responsibilities with respect to its use of intellectual property. Colleges and universities should expect to receive notice from rights holders that faculty, staff, or students have placed what the rights holder claims to be infringing copies of copyrighted materials on the network. Such claims must be handled promptly and responsibly, but the institution must consider open process, academic freedom, free speech, and fair use under copyright law as core institutional values. Advanced networks make available a much broader range of materials for network access. But as the new legislation makes clear, they also require heightened and scrupulous responsibility in making use of these opportunities. Academic libraries will play a key role in defining, structuring, and managing these responsibilities.

Conclusion

Networked information access, as enabled by today's commercial Internet or by new advanced networks of the future, offers tremendous benefits to higher education. Much more information will continue to be made much more accessible. This information will include digital analogues of today's print journals and access to an ever-growing amount of the historical scholarly record as captured in the book and journal literature. It will also include a wide range of new genres of scholarly communication that we are just beginning to understand, including scientific databases, collaboratory activities, digital video, and scholarly Web sites, which will build on and move beyond traditional scholarly publishing. Internet2 will play a key role in enabling new developments in these areas, many of which cannot be effectively supported by today's Internet.

The emerging world of networked information clearly will generate a wide range of new and important roles for college and university libraries. Academic libraries will take stewardship of their institutions' intellectual assets and will organize and preserve new electronic scholarly works. They will educate the academic community about the selection and evaluation of new resources. They will collaborate with authors in the areas of management and rights clearance. And they will be a focal point for institutional policy development and implementation regarding the use of copyrighted materials.

Although these exciting developments offer great opportunities for improving scholarship, research, teaching, and learning, they will offer little relief in the near term for the chronic budgetary problems facing academic libraries. To the extent that they do offer relief in this area, it will be in the form of improved access by smaller institutions and, perhaps, reductions in capital construction costs at larger schools, assuming that the academic community is prepared to accept electronic replacements for print collections. And the new technologies challenge all academic libraries to design programs and services that support the greater flexibility and accessibility (but also complexity) of the networked information environment, which also represents a real cost.

Much of the discussion to date about digital information has been dominated by research library concerns. Research libraries serve a unique clientele and have a very special, crucial, and complex mission within the research university and within society as a whole, and electronic information is an essential component of their evolving strategies—but only one component. As commercial offerings multiply and the use of networked information becomes better understood and more routine, it seems clear that new strategies will also become available for the broader academic library community. The strategic alternatives for college libraries may be quite different from those appropriate for research libraries. In fact, college libraries, if provided with an appropriate technology infrastructure, may be able to move more rapidly and comprehensively to exploit networked information opportunities. Senior executive officers at these institutions face strategic planning challenges in information technology, networking, distance education, and budget and finance. The choices and possibilities raised by networked information have significant implications for each of these areas.

References

Association of Research Libraries, Statistics and Measurement Program. [www.arl.org/stats/arlstat/1998t2.html]. 1998.
Pew Higher Education Round Table. "To Publish and Perish." *Policy Perspectives,* 1998, 7 (entire issue 4).

3

Inventing the Advanced Internet

Douglas E. Van Houweling

The Internet that is used today by millions of people around the world to send e-mail and to access the World Wide Web traces its technological roots back more than thirty years to the U.S. Department of Defense's ARPANET project. In 1986, the National Science Foundation's NSFNET, based on technology developed for the ARPANET, linked five national supercomputer centers; it quickly grew to connect every major university in the United States. As the NSFNET expanded to link university and college campuses, the networks on the campuses themselves expanded to connect larger and more diverse academic communities.

In many ways, the decommissioning of the NSFNET backbone network in 1995 hailed the beginning of the Internet as a commercial communications medium. Since then the Internet has grown far faster than any previous electronic medium, outstripping the growth of both radio and television. Since the first exchange between two computers in 1969 as part of the ARPANET, the Internet has grown to connect nearly one hundred million hosts. Perhaps more significantly, the amount of information transmitted over the Internet now doubles every one hundred days.

Despite its tremendous growth, some aspects of the Internet have remained remarkably constant. A significant portion of the Internet's underlying technology is still based on the technology developed as part of the ARPANET and NSFNET projects.

Throughout the development of the Internet, the most compelling network applications have enabled people to communicate with one another. For example, e-mail and the World Wide Web, both developed within the academic community, are now the most commonly used applications on the commercial Internet. The same capabilities used by researchers and educators in the past today allow Internet users to collaborate and communicate in ways not previously possible.

The compelling nature of communication it enables has led to the Internet's rapid growth and increasing commercial use. Moreover, Internet technology is the basis of a global, multibillion-dollar industry. During the mid-1990s, it became increasingly apparent that a new round of development was needed to extend the capabilities of the Internet to support its rapid expansion and reorientation from a research endeavor to a primarily commercial service. New underlying technology was needed not only to accommodate the increasing number of hosts attached to the network but also to enable applications such as real-time video that either worked poorly or did not work at all on the Internet.

With the explosion of the commercial Internet, individuals from the worlds of academe, industry, and government who had nurtured the Internet in its infancy began discussing the potential for another cycle of innovation. They envisioned technology and applications beyond the capacity of the current Internet that would be increasingly important to research, education, and, ultimately, commerce. However, the demands of the rapidly growing commercial Internet precluded the kind of research, development, and testing that would be needed before deploying these new capabilities. Whereas commercial interests were necessarily focusing on the next three to six months, developing the necessary technology would require looking ahead some three to six years.

Recognizing the limitations of the new commercial Internet for research and development, in 1995 the National Science Foundation (NSF) created a separate high-performance network called the vBNS (very-high-performance Backbone Network Service) between its (then) five supercomputer centers. Scientists using this network soon discovered that extensive changes throughout the system—not just faster "pipes"—would be required to achieve the kinds of performance envisioned for future science and engineering. At the same time, their early applications developed for this new system began to demonstrate how an advanced network can change the nature and organization of research. The NSF began the process of extending access to this network to leading research universities the following year, to involve a larger community in the quest for advanced networking.

Building on this vision and early experience, the Internet2 project was formed to facilitate the precommercial development of new Internet applications and technologies. Following a series of meetings, thirty-four universities announced Internet2 on October 1, 1996. Shortly thereafter, President Clinton unveiled the Next Generation Internet (NGI) initiative, a federally led networking development effort that drew together and expanded on work already under way at federal agencies. In the tradition of collaboration between higher education and the federal government in research and development, the two initiatives have from the outset worked closely together toward complementary goals. The individuals and organizations undertaking each initiative also clearly understand the importance of partnership with industry to ensure commercialization of the results of their work and have engaged leading companies in their efforts. In many important respects, Internet2 and NGI re-create the model that successfully developed the Internet we use today.

What Is Internet2?

Internet2 is enabling the development and deployment of advanced network applications for research and education. As a project that brings together higher education, industry, and government,

Internet2 is facilitating efforts among member organizations to re-create a leading-edge networking capability for the national research community. Internet2 is also keenly focused on rapidly transferring the new network services and applications developed as part of the project to the broader Internet community. Through the Internet2 project, university members are coordinating efforts to deploy advanced campus networks, establish high-performance connectivity among their campuses, and develop the advanced network services needed to enable advanced applications, such as *quality of service* (commonly called QoS) and *multicasting* (an efficient way to send the same information to many receivers at the same time).

Since it began in October 1996, the Internet2 project has grown to include over 150 universities, more than fifty companies, and dozens of other organizations focused on advanced networking. By October 1997 it had become clear that Internet2 would require a formal organization, and the University Corporation for Advanced Internet Development (UCAID) was established as a nonprofit corporate base. In April 1998 UCAID, working with corporate partners, initiated the Abilene project to develop a nationwide high-performance network in support of the Internet2 project. Working with other advanced research and development networks, Abilene provides a national test bed for the new technologies and advanced applications being developed as a part of Internet2.

Much of the work on the Internet2 project is taking place at member universities, which have both a keen interest in new network capabilities and an unsurpassed pool of networking talent. Universities also represent a very advanced set of users, ideally suited to using and testing developmental applications and technologies.

In fact, a defining characteristic of the Internet2 project is the extent to which member institutions are investing their own resources to achieve common goals. Participating in Internet2 provides an organization with the opportunity to engage in the development of the next generation of networking technologies. However, the considerable institutional commitment of resources the project requires may be beyond what is practical for every college and university (or, for that matter, every company). Although participating in Internet2 is for many as costly as participating in the initial development of the Internet was, a prime goal of the project is that the new technologies and applications it creates will be quickly deployed in the commercial network. Just as the cost of connecting to and using the Internet has dropped dramatically over the past decade, we expect a similar decline in the cost of using advanced network technologies and applications.

Though it is led by and focused on higher education, the Internet2 project will only realize its full potential by engaging many organizations from different sectors. Among the most important of these is industry. At the most basic level, corporate members of Internet2 have committed energy and resources to support the activities of Internet2 universities. However, the true depth of industry engagement in Internet2 is demonstrated by the ongoing two-way collaborations that are taking place between the various partners as part of the project. These include focused efforts to develop specific technologies or applications, such as improved quality of service and digital networked video. Active partnerships such as these will lay the foundation for quickly moving new technologies into the broader higher education and networking communities.

Fundamentally important to advanced networking is continued government support. Just as the success of the Internet depended on early and sustained investment by the federal government, Internet2 leverages the investment in research of initiatives such as NGI. For example, one part of the NGI program, the NSF vBNS, serves as one of the backbone networks for Internet2 universities. Grants from NSF's High Performance Connections program helped many Internet2 member institutions establish high-performance connectivity to support the kind of advanced applications that are at the heart of Internet2's mission. Another key consideration is the demonstrated power of the federal government to catalyze industry support in this area.

To foster sustained success for the global Internet, UCAID is forming international collaborations with similar organizations around the world. Partnership and collaboration with organizations devoted to advanced networking development will help ensure a global, interoperable networking infrastructure. These agreements also support collaboration within the international academic community by providing appropriate interconnection among advanced research and education networks worldwide. International collaboration will also accelerate the commercial availability of new services and applications throughout the global Internet.

Regional and national networking organizations have played a crucial role in supporting Internet2 efforts at universities. Regional networking consortia have been instrumental in establishing many of the advanced networking nodes known as gigaPoPs that connect groups of Internet universities. (See Chapter Five for a detailed discussion of the value of regional networking.) Both nationally and regionally, networking organizations play key roles in extending developments in advanced networking (and their implications) to a larger community of participants. In both cases, one of the most important links is to the broader community of education.

Advanced Networking Across Academic Institutions

In contrast to their counterparts in industry, specialists in a particular academic field are often located across the country at various institutions. Thus there is an especially strong need within the academic community for technologies that allow scholars to collaborate at a distance. Universities are also home to leading experts in many areas of networking research and development. As a result, university members of the Internet2 project are investing considerable resources on each of their campuses to develop and deploy advanced network technology and applications.

Advanced networking has the potential to transform how higher education accomplishes its research and education missions. More precisely, revolutionary applications, taking advantage of widely deployed advanced networking capabilities, will enable completely new ways of conducting research, teaching, and learning. From her office workstation, a professor will be able to access CD-quality digital audio libraries located across campus as if they were on her desktop. From his laboratory, a researcher will be able to access and control a telescope located across the country. From her own lecture hall, a student will be able to interact with a group of students located at institutions around the world as if they were in the same room.

As one of the first steps toward realizing this promise, Internet2 universities are currently building campus networks to provide the capacity these new applications will need. They are also establishing high-capacity connections to high-performance backbone networks so that they can use these applications across their campuses. Though they are joined together in the common goals of the Internet2 project, each institution is determining the types of investments necessary on its own campus to implement the network upgrades. Satellite-based and terrestrial wireless networks further expand the possibilities.

But wide deployment of advanced applications requires a framework of tools and capabilities on top of the physical network infrastructure. This loose collection of tools, called *middleware*, performs such crucial functions as verifying user identification and authorizing access to on-line resources. Middleware is also needed in areas such as directory services, accounting systems, and network operation and management. Developing standards-based middleware to ensure network security is a priority as the Internet is increasingly being used across multiple institutions. This is especially true for administrative purposes in the academic community and electronic commerce in the business world.

Today, many advanced applications can operate within the bounds of a laboratory or on a single campus. Many of these have already been demonstrated at Internet2 events. As an advanced networking infrastructure is extended on campuses and more extensive middleware is developed and deployed within that infrastructure, advanced applications will be widely adopted by research and education activities, in a range of content areas and contexts.

Getting Ready for Advanced Networking

As a research and development project, Internet2 is focused on new technologies and applications that will, when proven, be deployed throughout the Internet. The developmental nature of the project and the significant investment required to participate means that not every institution of higher education will join Internet2. However, understanding the significance of advanced networking capabilities for education and research, Internet2 and partner organizations are working to ensure that the benefits of new network technologies and applications are as broadly available and applicable as possible, as quickly as possible.

Links between Internet2 and national higher education and networking organizations provide a means to share information about networking development broadly. Internet2 is working with organizations such as the Association of American Universities, the American Association for the Advancement of Science, the Coalition for Networked Information, EDUCAUSE, and the National Association of State Universities and Land-Grant Colleges to promote communication with the national education and research communities. The value of advanced networking to higher education will be realized when it moves beyond the computer science and information technology disciplines to fields such as biology, political science, and the performing arts.

Significant regional collaborations through Internet2 gigaPoPs and individual Internet2 universities are already providing similar information and technology transfer opportunities. Organizational and network links often already exist between institutions participating directly in the development of advanced networking, other higher education institutions, K–12 institutions, and local, state, and regional organizations. These links provide for the diffusion today of information and technologies that will help prepare organizations to adopt advanced network applications and technology tomorrow, as they become more widely accessible.

The extent to which industry and the commercial Internet adopt new network technologies and applications will perhaps be one of the most important indicators of the project's long-term success. Higher education is a distributed community that uses networking to work with organizations around the world. In fact, around 80 percent of network traffic from the campuses of U.S. universities flows to organizations outside the university community. This high level of interaction with a wide range of organizations, combined with the importance to research and education of the capabilities enabled by advanced networking, requires that advanced networking be made as broadly available in the future as the commercial Internet is today. When the global commercial Internet we all use begins to integrate the advanced networking capabilities needed to enable everyone to use revolutionary applications, research and education will benefit.

Digital Video: Imminent Convergence

Convergence, or the unified delivery of services such as text, voice, video, and data that we now consider distinct, is widely anticipated as an imminent result of the rise of the Internet. Today's global Internet, however, is not able to support services such as voice or video with the quality we have come to expect from telephones and televisions. Even with a high-speed connection, the underlying technology usually limits video transmitted over the Internet in real time to a postage-stamp-sized window with clipped audio. Anything larger requires a long download, and the user must then play the video back from local storage. The Internet2 digital video initiative (I2–DV) aims to develop technology that will allow ubiquitous, high-quality digital video and audio to be transmitted over the network in real time.

This initiative seeks to do far more than just provide "TV over the Internet," however. Its goal is to enable a whole range of computer applications in which video is simply part of the application. Streaming one-way video, in real time or delayed, as well as interactive two-way video will be integrated into applications in a wide range of contexts. High-definition video with high-fidelity, multi-channel audio will be available to individuals, pairs of people, or large groups communicating simultaneously.

The capabilities envisioned by the Internet2 digital video initiative are especially relevant for higher education. Colleges and universities already produce video content in the course of their research and education activities. Even developing the tools to manage existing resources for accessing and archiving information is a serious challenge. Furthermore, since a major goal of Internet2 is to transfer new capabilities to the commercial Internet, I2–DV will work to enable the distribution of high-quality digital video beyond those campuses with connections to high-performance networks.

Most exciting are the new opportunities for research and education that will be created as a result of the new capabilities being developed as part of this initiative. Ubiquitous digital video will provide new options for teaching and learning, for conducting research, and for clinical practice. Remote instruments, such as electron microscopes and high-performance telescopes, will be accessible over the network from across the country. Communities of researchers and scholars will collaborate without leaving their own campuses. The best students in a highly specialized discipline will meet and study together as if they were in the same classroom.

Yet, even a cursory survey of the I2–DV vision reveals significant technical challenges. These extend from the way digital video content will be generated, manipulated, and distributed to how users will find, access, and display it. Tools for capturing, editing, and merging content from multiple sources need to be developed and must take into account a wide variety of display technologies, including three-dimensional immersive environments and even direct retinal projection. The current patchwork of vendor-specific schemes for encoding, storing, and serving digital video content needs to be merged into the kind of interoperable environment that has been a hallmark of successful Internet applications such as e-mail and the Web.

There are an equal number of challenges in developing the underlying network services and technologies necessary to provide the kind of network performance required to transmit high-quality video. Quality-of-service and multicasting technologies will help allocate network resources more efficiently. A broad range of middleware, such as authentication, authorization, resource scheduling, and content-searching facilities, needs to be developed. These challenges will be addressed within the broader Internet2 project, working with existing standards-setting bodies and industry members to ensure the development of interoperable technologies in each of these areas.

To meet the challenges of enabling the widespread deployment of advanced digital video, I2–DV is bringing together communities from academe, industry, and government. New services driving the development of technology within I2–DV will provide test beds for the commercial Internet. Virtual conferencing, "netcasting," digital production and content services, and listing and search services—all focused on the needs of higher education—will serve as models and proof-of-concept for similar services that will start to be deployed as the commercial Internet begins incorporating the underlying technologies needed to support them.

Although the initial steps in the Internet2 digital video initiative are already being taken today, the project's broad scope means that its effects on the commercial Internet will only begin to be felt several years from now. An important aspect of both I2–DV and the Internet2 project is their ability to provide a window into the future. Internet2 allows a glimpse of the high-performance environment of tomorrow's Internet, its effect on human interaction, and its potential to join people and communities.

Conclusion

Just as the tremendous success of the Internet has been based on its ability to let people communicate in revolutionary new ways, the Internet2 project will ultimately succeed to the extent that it lets people accomplish the previously impossible. Capabilities that not long ago were used by just a handful of scientists are today transforming the way we all work, learn, and live. Researchers working on Internet2 today to make electron microscopes remotely accessible, to extend the reach of digital video libraries, and to enable atmospheric scientists to collaborate over a distance will again revolutionize the way we all communicate. By staying a step ahead of currently available commercial networking, and through the continual development and use of advanced networking, the Internet2 project will help ensure that higher education will continue to have access to the latest technology.

4

Planning, Designing, and Growing a Campus Network for the Future

Philip E. Long

The campus network has become a core infrastructure for teaching, learning, and research in higher education. All of the many electronic teaching, library, and administrative services of an institution of higher education are built on top of and assume the existence of a ubiquitous, capacious, reliable campus network. How can a college or university create such a network? And once created, how can it be managed and maintained? With the rapid advances in networking technology—real-time video and services not yet even imagined—how can a school keep up and be prepared for the unknown? This chapter has some good news to share: by following some basic guidelines, a campus can ensure network growth and renewal, providing continual network upgrades and maintaining a position of flexibility to meet expected and unexpected future needs.

This good news about campus computer networks is easy to understand. Campus needs and computer network technologies are both changing continually, so campus network planning must be an ongoing project. Likewise, rapid change and growth in demand means the network itself must undergo constant upgrades and renewals. Data networks have been around long enough, changing continually, that the industry has developed a standard set of high-level-design building blocks and practices that the most basic network shares with the most complex. Also, this substantial experience has enabled the development of a set of guiding principles for designing and managing networks to maximize returns on investment and promote flexibility to meet changing needs. The key to having a campus network that will maintain its currency and gracefully accommodate future advanced services is to use these building blocks and principles to guide ongoing renewals that maximize network value, technology, and flexibility.

Another piece of good news: once a certain critical mass is achieved with a standards-guided campus network, unit costs will level off, even in the face of continued rapid expansion in connections or bandwidth. Because of rising user expectations and some external influences, however, overall network costs are likely to continue to rise at rates substantially above inflation for the foreseeable future. Specialized applications beyond the mainstream will require specialized equipment and knowledge and thus will come at a premium cost (though they will likely use standard network building blocks and cabling). But that cost need only be incurred when the service need is demonstrated and justifies the expenditure.

A set of external factors do have the potential to disrupt this fairly rosy picture, but there is reason to hope that a soundly designed campus network will even be able to address the next network revolution akin to the 1994 arrival of the World Wide Web.

Guiding Principles for Network Planning and Design

A set of principles to guide the design, management, and evolution of even highly complex high-speed networks has evolved based on experience with both small and large networks. These principles are not inviolable, of course, but a network designer or campus manager should nevertheless question any proposed exceptions to them. The following principles are characteristics of the best networks of all sizes in higher education and beyond. Each of these principles is illustrated with examples in the follow-up discussion of network building blocks.

- *Planning should be ongoing.* Because campus needs and network technologies are changing continually, planning must be ongoing. Typically there should be a yearly update of the overall network plan and technical standards.

- *Network designs should be based on standard building blocks.* Designing around the standard, replaceable network building blocks is critical and should be the routine practice. Existing networks will already conform in most if not all ways to the standard building blocks. Both design and building blocks are standard only at a high level and still need careful mapping to local building structures and campus needs. Commercial products will fit and support these standard designs and building blocks.

  A corollary to this principle is the principle that good design minimizes costs. Networks are extraordinarily complex technical enterprises; bad design (for example, not observing the building blocks) quickly promotes very high operating and management costs.

- *Network costs are operating costs, not capital costs.* All networks need ongoing renewal; except for laying pathway and cabling, maintaining a network is an operating cost, not a capital cost! This is probably the most frequently violated principle. A close corollary to this principle is the "no free lunch" principle, which states that every addition of capacity or function to even a well-designed network does cost something, both to accomplish and to maintain.

- *Networks should be continually renewed.* Because networks are still growing rapidly in terms of numbers of users, speed and capacity, services, and reliability, they are subject to constant changes in ways small and large.

The key to establishing and maintaining a quality network is to use those ongoing changes to provide continual upgrades within the scope of a periodically
updated plan.

- *Networks should grow gracefully.* Following these principles when constructing initially small networks allows
  such networks to evolve more or less seamlessly into
  more complex, higher-speed networks that can fully
  support advanced services when they are needed.

- *Network investments should be value based.* Investment
  in network building blocks has a significant influence
  on future flexibility and costs. Investment should be
  proportional to the expected life span, allow for cost
  trends, and recognize that opportunity costs can easily
  dominate marginal cost. The shorter the life span for a
  particular network element, the closer capacity should
  be to actual need; the longer the life span, the more
  that overcapacity is appropriate. If costs are dropping
  over time, investment should be close to actual need; if
  costs are rising, investment should usually include extra
  capacity. Opportunity costs may justify overcapacity;
  for example, marginal materials costs may be quite low
  to provide extra capacity.

  Note that the "no free lunch" principle reminds us
  that all capacity incurs some level of ongoing maintenance, so overcapacity plans should always be related
  directly to identifiable and anticipated campus needs,
  recognizing the carrying costs.

- *Networks should use commodity goods.* Wherever possible, commodity goods should be used; commercial
  trends drive prices down and encourage innovation to
  extend the life and utility of common commercial
  products.

- *Networks should use open standards.* Wherever functional needs can be met, open standards should be adopted and proprietary standards avoided. This is the commodity goods principle applied to software. The Internet community will use and develop open standards, which will provide lower cost and higher innovation than an individual company or set of companies can achieve with proprietary protocols.

- *Networks require active management.* A network is a highly complex technical enterprise and can only meet predictable service standards if it is engineered from the ground up to provide management data and error reports and to permit active probing and management by network administrators.

- *Networks need appropriate redundancy.* Network plans should provide for a level of redundancy appropriate for the number of nodes or the amount of capacity that would be disabled by a particular network element failure. Note that as campus expectations for reliability rise, the level of redundancy needed will rise correspondingly. The "no free lunch" principle reminds us that although redundancy may be necessary to meet reliability goals, it adds complexity to a network and thus raises costs, so it should be added wisely.

- *Outsourcing should be used judiciously.* A campus should generally have full control over issues that directly affect its programs, but it often makes sense to leave nonprogrammatic issues to others. Thus commodity services can be outsourced, but management of program services should be retained internally. Data network functions are still critical to the ongoing and rapid development of program-related activities such as providing access to library materials, distance education, and administrative streamlining, so few campuses currently consider outsourcing the core design and management of their data network (as they might, for example, for their phone network). The use of off-the-shelf components within standard designs provides some benefits similar to outsourcing. And many campuses are outsourcing network services that have standard interfaces to the campus network and that are undergoing rapid commercialization or innovation (for example, remote network access). Any outsourcing arrangement requires careful management to ensure that campus program needs drive the services.

Assembling Networks from Standard Building Blocks

At a high level, a campus network consists of precisely defined functional layers that build from the physical infrastructure to the network applications. Each of the three layers relies on the layer below it (layering is simplified).

1. The physical layer includes the physical plant that carries the electrical signals—the conduit through which the cabling runs (pathway) and the cable itself.

2. The network layer includes protocols and electronics that turn electrical signals into messages—the network hubs, switches, routers, gateways, firewalls, and computer network interface cards that assign names and addresses to devices on the network and govern how messages are passed.

3. The applications layer includes network applications that turn messages into services. Core network applications include electronic mail, directories, Web servers and browsers, and so forth.

Each of these layers is composed of standard building blocks (examples are provided in the section on network design). The simplest local area network connecting three machines to a printer uses these layers and basic building blocks, and so do the most advanced campus networks.

The Importance of Ongoing Planning

Each of a network's standard building blocks has a finite useful life, after which it must be renewed. Guided by an overall plan, individual building blocks can be renewed to upgrade and improve each of the areas over time, providing gradual improvement in function and capacity across the entire network in the normal course of maintenance. This is one of many reasons why appropriate and ongoing planning is absolutely essential to creating and maintaining a quality campus network.

A quality planning process is essential for an enterprise that is growing and changing quickly. Without quality planning (and execution), the network will quickly lose its coherence; with good planning (and execution), the network can be made to serve current needs well and evolve gracefully and cost-effectively to meet future needs, even those that cannot yet be anticipated. Planning must, first and foremost, be anchored in a campus's specific network needs. Planning must be technically competent and informed by current industry and campus practice and trends. Planning must also develop campus buy-in through community involvement in the planning process, typically via advisory committees, and full disclosure of the planning process and plans to the community.

Critical success factors for network planning include good technical planning (concerning function, capacity, reliability, scaling, and security), end-user support, a cost and funding model, network policies, community communication, and network expertise. Given the rapid change in every aspect of data networks, the plan needs to be reviewed and updated annually in terms of all of the critical success factors.

Technical Planning

Evaluation of the technical issues of function, capacity, reliability, scaling, and security typically involve steps such as the following:

1. Develop a network profile based on historical data of number of connections, traffic patterns, and other standard technical measures. What has been the pattern of growth, and what might the future look like?

2. Identify known problems in the local network, such as congestion or reliability problems.

3. Assess changing user and institutional expectations and functional and service needs. Are end users' expectations for service changing? What new services will be needed to support, for example, a new distance education plan?

4. Review local and national network growth and trends, especially at similar schools.

5. Identify changing technology opportunities and options. Might new technologies meet particular campus needs?

The update of the technical plan will draw directly on these considerations. It also needs to include network management—active monitoring of network components, gathering of usage statistics, response to failures, and so forth—in addition to the traffic patterns and performance of the actual network.

End-User Support

Most schools recognize that providing end-user support is essential to a successful network. As campus networks become more mature, the responsibility for helping end users solve network problems has gradually shifted from the staff who design and operate the network to those who assist users with the academic and administrative application systems that use the network. Whatever the approach on a given campus, no network can be successful if end users do not have a clear point of contact to turn to in case of problems.

Cost and Funding Models

Appropriate allocation of funding and costs is obviously critical. This issue is the one most likely to reflect local culture and practice and thus to differ from school to school. However, a few comments may be helpful. Most planners expect that, once mature, the data network funding and cost allocation model will parallel how the campus manages its telephone costs. But current networks are still expanding rapidly in terms of number of connections, capacity, expectations, and standards for reliability, so their cost basis is still rising rapidly, and the network funding plan must address this reality. Managing the network to minimize expenses consistent with service expectations is critical.

The value-based investment principle reminds us that it is important not to overbuy networking capacity, because capacity unneeded this year will usually be available at less cost next year when it *is* needed. But this analysis will vary across the standard building blocks. Some external factors affect network costs as well; for example, security attacks and the cost of defending against them are escalating rapidly. A successful network will be based on an honest network funding model that is consistent with the local campus culture and that addresses rising campus needs and expectations for network reliability and capacity with new investments and reallocations that may well exceed the growth of normal campus budgets.

Network Policies

Policies for appropriate use are critical to a well-managed campus network, and evolving network functions do affect these policies, requiring periodic reviews of them. For example, the recent upswing in security attacks has led some schools to consider scanning their networks for security vulnerabilities. Current network policies may not permit this, however. EDUCAUSE maintains links to many campus network–related policies that can be used as examples in creating or updating such policies (www.educause.edu/issues/policy.html).

Community Communication

Although many schools formally publish their technical network plan, most end users will not have read it. Thus a growing method for informing the community about current network services is to provide *service level agreements*, which lay out for end users what functions they can expect, with what level of capacity, reliability, security, and support, and at what cost. Such agreements provide the essence of the network plan (from the end user's point of view). Of course, it is also critical to continue to publish the complete technical network plan.

Network Expertise

Two key challenges arise with respect to network expertise: how can you get help if you don't currently have the capability to design and plan a network, and how can you develop the networking staff that you do have?

The planning and design of a campus network is too important a job to outsource completely, considering both the program implications of the network and the reality that it will need to be guided by a plan that evolves smoothly over time. But this is also too important a function to entrust entirely to local staff if they are not yet ready to manage it successfully. Many campuses have successfully created a robust campus network planning process that fully involves local technical staff under the oversight of a competent project manager. This approach brings in a network consultant to "jump start" the planning process. The goal is not to rely on the consultant to do the planning, but rather to employ him or her to guide the process and provide initial technical advice.

Another source of help is to review model campus network solutions. EDUCAUSE periodically identifies model campus networks through its network award program (www.educause.edu/awards/network/network-award.html), and many schools present their network plans and strategies at conferences sponsored by or affiliated with EDUCAUSE or other technology-related associations (www.educause.edu/conference/conf.html). Finally, the usual practice of visiting two or three peer schools known to have developed successful networks is another useful tactic.

The challenge of recruiting, developing, and retaining qualified staff is as critical for the network as for any technical area. Ongoing training is essential for all technical staff and is a foundation for development and retention. Staff development costs include both dollars and time, but the alternative to incurring these costs is simply unacceptable. Training opportunities arise on a continuum, from individual study (through vendor certification and commercial self-study programs) to targeted networking workshops and conferences, user groups, visits to peer schools with similar but perhaps slightly greater networking challenges, formal courses lasting up to a week or even longer, and reading papers and articles about networking written by colleagues. EDUCAUSE maintains a Web-based library of abstracted and indexed articles, conference papers, campus plans and policies, and other information, searchable by topic and keyword (www.educause.edu/ir/ir-library.html). As is true for any investment, management must work with staff to identify training that is appropriate to each individual's current skills and future responsibilities.

The Guiding Principles at Work in Network Design

The guiding principles outlined earlier can be applied to every aspect of network design and management. The following discussion illustrates a few of the principles (continuous renewal, commodity goods, graceful growth, active management, and open standards) in action on several of the core standard building blocks—pathway, station and interbuilding cabling, network electronics, and network protocols.

Pathway

Buried (in walls and underground) pathway is the most difficult network element to add or modify. Pathway has the longest useful life of any network element, on the order of the life of a building—certainly twenty or even fifty years.

With respect to *value-based investment*, pathway entails generally high construction costs, which usually increase at at least the rate of inflation, and high opportunity costs for construction (a project is expensive to initiate). However, once construction is under way, marginal costs to provide extra capacity (more pathway) are usually low. For these reasons, constructing adequate buried pathway when the opportunity arises is critical, and it makes sense to overbuild to provide maximum future flexibility. Spare pathway ensures the potential to adjust wired networks to future developments. A rough formula for overbuilding of pathway is to estimate the maximum concretely foreseeable use and double it.

With respect to *continuous renewal* analysis, pathway within a building is most easily renewed when a building is renovated. Older buildings, constructed when the telephone was the communications standard, may need a significant (costly) construction project to add pathway, typically by running up elevator shafts, through closets, or through or over walls. Such construction is often done in conjunction with other building system renewal projects, such as the addition of sprinkler systems. Pathway between buildings rarely needs to be renewed but periodically may need to be supplemented, typically on the same cycle as building renovation (twenty to twenty-five years).

Station and Interbuilding Cabling

All cabling projects should consider telephone and cable TV needs as well as data transmission needs, and different kinds of conduit are often pulled or even cabled together. To be consistent, this discussion focuses only on data transmission cable, but similar principles apply to planning other cabling.

Station cabling is the cabling within a building that connects a wall plate in a room to the nearest telecommunications center (wiring center) where connections are made to network electronics or to cables to other buildings. *Interbuilding cabling* is the cabling that runs between buildings. Both elements have a long useful life—ten years or more—but even so they will eventually need to be renewed. A key point is that the most common problem with network planning is misunderstanding or not taking seriously the useful life of cabling and other components and failing to plan to renew them at the end of that useful life.

Applying the guiding principles to cabling involves a balancing act, considering both the very long useful life characteristic of pathway and the short life and frequent technology changes characteristic of network electronics (discussed next).

Network Electronics

Network electronics are the electrical devices that turn cables into a network (for example, Ethernet hubs and switches). Because they are essentially specialty computers, network electronics evolve quickly, improve in price and performance quickly, and have a correspondingly short useful life, typically only three years.

In terms of *value-based investment*, network electronics can be quite easily replaced with new electronics to provide faster speed or other improvements, assuming the network protocols do not change. Individual units can be replaced, providing new functionality or service to one subset of the campus network without requiring changes to the rest of the network and usually without requiring changes to end-user machines.

With respect to the principles of continuous renewal, commodity goods, and graceful growth, the real risk in investing in new network electronics is the possibility of a change to a new network protocol; such a change would require the simultaneous replacement of an entire set of network electronics in both the network and the end-user computers. Such a concern arose in 1996 and 1997 over the alleged end of the life of Ethernet. Ethernet was clearly aging and could not deliver the guaranteed bandwidth needed by advanced network applications, such as real-time digital video. Was it time to migrate to a new standard, such as asynchronous transfer mode (ATM)?

Because the Ethernet market was huge, the commodity goods principle drove the market to provide greatly improved Ethernet electronics at very low costs. These improvements became available for easy upgrades, without requiring end users to change their existing Ethernet interfaces (using switching technology). Furthermore, new machines with higher-speed interfaces can easily coexist on the same network (illustrating the principle of graceful growth). This was and is a huge win for network designers and end users and illustrates the substantial power of the market and the commodity goods principle. As electronics are replaced at the end of their useful life, the new equipment provides higher speed, more reliability, and more manageability at the same or lower unit cost!

In terms of the active management principle, all network electronics should have industry-standard management capability, and the principle of appropriate redundancy informs overall network design. Based on campus need for reliability, individual points of failure will be avoided by providing redundant cable paths, network electronics, staffing, and so on.

Higher-speed and specialized electronics such as ATM will be important for particular applications (for example, high-performance computation centers), but these services run over the standard cabling building blocks and thus can be easily installed when and where they are needed.

Network Protocols

When it comes to the open standards principle, IP wins! IP is the network protocol underlying the Internet; essentially all network-based applications are converting to run over IP networks. There is no need to consider other protocols for the foreseeable future. This provides an excellent example of how quality open standards outperform proprietary standards for mainstream needs.

Looking at this industry-standard protocol through the lens of the commodity goods principle, network electronics are commodity goods, and prices for hubs, switches, bridges, routers, and so forth track along the lines of the fast improvement of hardware price and performance.

In terms of the continuous renewal principle, a new version of the Internet protocol, IP V6, will gradually phase in to increase capacity and management options in IP networks, but this introduction will coexist with existing networks, allowing network managers to plan this upgrade in the natural course of network renewal.

External Factors Could Disrupt This Rosy Picture

A set of issues have the potential to disrupt the graceful growth of campus networks, including increasing costs and scarcity of qualified network staff, increasing security demands, and the next "killer application" that produces a discontinuity between user demands and network services.

Costs and Scarcity of Qualified Network Staff

The continued explosive growth of data networks, particularly in the commercial sector, has created huge demands for qualified network staff, bidding up wages and creating staff scarcities. Market trends suggest this scarcity is not likely to ease in the foreseeable future. It is critical, therefore, to organize data networks (using standards) to minimize dependence on individuals, minimize the need for scarce staff, and allow newly hired staff to become fully productive quickly. Other standard measures for developing and retaining professional staff, such as ensuring strong support for training in return for employee commitment to continued service, are also critical.

Increasing Security Demands

The Internet has become a full-fledged commercial environment, supporting the routine exchange of huge amounts of money and mission-critical information. Unfortunately, it has consequently come under attack by individuals determined to steal from companies transacting business on-line or to disrupt others' work. At the same time, the Internet community has expanded, including the number of persons willing to launch such attacks, and some individuals have developed highly sophisticated tool kits to make such attacks very easy. Although higher education institutions are not generally targeted by on-line thieves, every school has seen a rapid rise in network-related security incidents and concomitant losses of machine use, staff time, and data. Ongoing attention to machine and network security is now necessary for the entire array of networked machines; without adequate security, a network will be subject to disruption at unpredictable and certainly inconvenient times.

Killer Applications

Possible killer applications include full-motion digital video, voice communication over the data network (sometimes called *IP telephony* or *voice over IP*), and a shift in the underlying network to support guaranteed response (such as is needed for real-time process control). Full-motion digital video will require prodigious bandwidth. Will its inevitable arrival "break" our current networks? Or will computing power and compression technology improve fast enough that full-motion video will be easily supported over existing Ethernet connections (with an expanded network core)? Current thinking is that a combination of all of the above will apply, requiring an upgrade to the network's core capacity and upgrades to fast Ethernet in particularly sensitive locations but not fundamentally breaking the graceful growth of well-designed networks.

Supporting telephone service over the campus data network presents issues of reliability rather than bandwidth. Telephone communications should consume relatively modest bandwidth and should be easily accommodated by modern data networks, but the telephone system's reliability standard is "five 9s" (99.999 percent) uptime. Current data networking is nowhere near meeting this standard. What would it cost to meet this standard? Probably more than would justify migrating to over-network telephone communications for some time! A slow migration will provide time for networks to adjust gracefully.

The ability to provide guaranteed service was a primary consideration in the debate discussed earlier over a possible need to migrate from Ethernet to a new protocol, such as ATM. The commodity goods principle has already driven Ethernet to meet currently foreseeable needs, so such a protocol shift is not likely at the moment. But similar pressures will only grow more intense, likely driving further expansion using existing network models.

It is difficult to foresee killer applications, by their very definition. A killer application is likely to emerge again in the next five to ten years, just as the World Wide Web did five years ago. When it does, assuming the standard building-block design does not change, pathway needs and cabling demands will not change radically, although a new killer application could accelerate a migration from copper to fiber wiring. What is most likely to change are network electronics, the number of cables used, and possibly network interface equipment in the computers themselves. All of these are subject to regular change anyway. A well-designed network should be able to accommodate these changes more or less gracefully, possibly with an extra infusion of capital to accelerate turnover of equipment or to add new cables.

The best model of a mature data network is probably an analogue in many ways of the modern telephone system. In terms of overall network capacity compared to that of individual instruments, in terms of reliability, and in terms of function, the campus network still has much room to grow and mature. But we have enough history to imagine the future in many ways as a logical extension of the past, and that experience can help guide a graceful evolution.

Conclusion

The good news is that there is nothing mysterious about preparing a college or university for a networked future: a campus network can develop and grow according to well-understood principles, in an orderly, well-coordinated process of planning and implementation. Today's campus leader, although having little other need to be an expert in networking technology, must nevertheless take a personal interest in it to ensure that this happens.

5

Working with Your Neighbors

Ron Hutchins

Effective long-term relationships between universities, community colleges, K–12 school systems, and other educational institutions are growing in importance. Today *virtual communities* are forming across and among these sectors through computer networks to share ideas, expertise, academic resources, and professional support for specific challenges. Even though these institutions in some ways may compete for students, grants, acclaim, and financial support, an awareness is developing that the ultimate success of each institution will depend to a high degree on the strength and reach of its ongoing partnerships and collaborations with others.

On a more practical level, severe constraints on both budgets and expert personnel provide compelling reasons to collaborate on the development and operation of the expensive network infrastructure needed by all institutions and to spread the monetary investment in these areas across as many users and applications as possible. Building partnerships and collaborations, both formal and informal, between research and education institutions can create the critical technical, intellectual, and financial capital required to move into the next century of technology.

This chapter addresses

- Ways in which regional, national, and international collaborations can multiply both personal and institutional opportunities in higher education

- The special roles that advanced state and regional networks and connection points (sometimes called gigaPoPs) can play in supporting the development of advanced networking among member institutions

- The enabling role of regional networks in transforming the educational community

Relationships, Communities, and Networks

Needs and opportunities create relationships, ongoing relationships create communities, and networks (whether human or technological) facilitate and mediate those relationships. Specific networks are typically developed to support the communication needs of an existing or desired community. Once in place, however, the same networks enable the creation of additional communities that would not have formed had they not been able to easily communicate. This unplanned multiplier effect must be a critical part of any discussion about networking the higher education community.

The Power of Networked Communities

Let's first take a look at some of the communities whose relationships have been instrumental in motivating regional, national, and international networking.

The Physics Community

This community is made up of a small, international group of physicists who collaborate closely in the development and use of very specialized and expensive laboratory facilities. Creating the combined infrastructure to support such experiments simply would not be possible without such global collaboration. Some experiments may last two years or more in tightly controlled facilities that are scheduled around the clock. Yet *virtual* access to this complex infrastructure through international communications networks can permit monitoring and control from any site with sufficient network capabilities. Beyond the savings in lost time and travel, this approach can speed and improve the magnitude and quality of the entire research effort by opening participation to a much wider set of experts and students.

The Atmospheric Sciences Community

Observation and data collection facilities are operated around the globe to allow twenty-four-hour study of phenomena such as weather and sunspots. Some of these facilities must be located in hostile or very inaccessible environments to collect the appropriate data. Taken together, the required instruments are beyond the budget of any single organization. Yet by connecting all the instruments to a global network, atmospheric scientists at many different locations can collaborate on collecting and sharing valuable information. Moreover, the ability to collect and analyze data captured simultaneously across wide regions enables scientists to create huge "virtual instruments" that can tackle problems that could not otherwise be solved. As with the physics community, networking captures the intellectual contributions of a wider scientific community and strengthens the entire process of discovery. Connecting these sites together via communications networks has fundamentally changed the way atmospheric science is done.

Institutional Collaborations

Existing academic relationships within regions have led to the creation of virtual communities through participation in common regional networks. In a large Midwestern consortium of twelve research universities called the Committee for Inter-institutional Cooperation (CIC), formal relationships dating back to 1958 between provosts and other academic officers have resulted in a number of courses that are shared between the member institutions, using various forms of electronic communications. The same association has also forged an alliance that effectively unites their library holdings into a much larger whole. These new services and relationships are moving increasingly onto the Internet as well, as it reaches sufficient levels of performance. Advanced networks will eventually unify their various technological underpinnings into a single system.

University Systems

The University of California is building a single new digital library to serve the needs of all of its campuses and numerous partners. The success of this approach will depend on the availability of capable, advanced networks to link the members. One such network, called CENIC, is now under active development. In other regions, such as the state of Iowa, state government has played an active role in developing large networks that connect multiple sectors of the education community. Although such networks may initially support the wider sharing of instruction, professional development, library resources, and administrative services that were previously conducted on special-purpose networks, they soon lead to a much richer set of services and relationships that span the entire community. Each of the communities mentioned previously has also played an active role in the technical and professional development its members require to take advantage of their new opportunities.

College Course Communities

In any university or college, a single discipline, course, or class can be thought of as a community. In a single class, the teacher sustains a one-to-many relationship with his or her students, and groups of students maintain many-to-many relationships with one another. In many colleges today, customized lists of electronic mail addresses, called Internet mailing lists, are used to broadcast messages to the members of a class (one to many, or even many to many), keeping all students abreast of current information, assignments, questions, and help. E-mail supports one-to-one relationships, letting teachers interact with students directly and privately. Internet newsgroups are another tool, used to publish ongoing discussions among students and teachers and maintain a trail of who said what and when, for continuity and future reference. Students use these tools spontaneously to form smaller study groups and work on assigned team projects. The same tools that work on a campus serve as well for additional students at remote sites, or even for "virtual classes" with students distributed across a region. This point brings us full circle—educational content and services delivered locally through the campus network can be delivered just as easily throughout a region, a nation, or the whole world.

The Multiplier Value of Unplanned Benefits

Networks are purposefully designed to support specific communities and relationships. Once established, however, networks often fill other, unanticipated roles. Most meetings and conferences are human networking events, designed for a very specific purpose—usually to exchange information on a single topic or at least related topics within a specialized community. It is widely agreed, however, that side conversations and hallway interactions among participants may be the most important part of such meetings.

The ARPANET, an early precursor of the Internet that was developed by the Advanced Research Projects Agency of the U.S. Department of Defense, was originally created to support specific research within the defense community. Once this networked community reached a (small) critical mass, "electronic hallway conversations" soon led to the evolution of new communities, based on the new ease with which their participants could communicate. Internet newsgroups and electronic mail, originally created to support the primary mission of the ARPANET, served the new communities just as well. The members of these new communities were largely self-selected. They wished to share resources (equipment, expertise, technical and managerial support), share ideas (data, information, hypotheses, discoveries), share experiences (specific problems and their resolutions), support broader communications and public relations (issues, positions, opinions), and transfer knowledge between members and to others outside the group.

The technical hierarchy of today's advanced data communications networks often mirrors the relationships invested in the underlying human networks. Libraries, laboratories, research consortia, and large networks for research (such as the vBNS network of the National Science Foundation, the Abilene network of the University Corporation for Advanced Internet Development, the ESNET of the Department of Energy, and the NSI network of the National Aeronautics and Space Administration) often have specific sponsors and a primary mission, usually to support a virtual community of scholars in a broad subject area. As with the ARPANET, however, the participants in these networks often build new virtual communities that may bridge the primary networks, resulting in powerful, creative forces in the evolution of research and education. This expanding functionality of networks has been recognized as one of the great success stories of the NSFNET and the others, and it must not be minimized when discussing the value of future network investments.

Why Bigger Really Is Better

Since networks can be very sensitive to economies of scale, campuses may benefit from regional networks, which can operate like buying clubs, providing increased value for their members' expenditures. As particular advanced services eventually become commodity goods, the need for a specific "buying club" may disappear. But the next set of advanced services required by the community often will follow a similar development cycle and will be better leveraged because of successful past collaborations.

Working in communities of interest also gives network designers and providers a larger base of customers with common needs. Both start-up and mature companies can work to satisfy these needs, with some expectation to get a return on their investment. For example, hardware and software development for multicast network services, which provide an efficient way of delivering the same data to many different destinations, is being driven in part by the expressed needs of the higher education community to support affordable distance learning. Although such arrangements may reduce costs, their greatest benefit may be greater and accelerated innovation and the commercial introduction of new services.

Networking customers, unlike consumers in many other areas, gain a double advantage as the price per unit declines. This is because the network becomes more valuable to each customer as more are connected. The total connected customer base is the population in which you can easily collaborate and from which you can conveniently build virtual communities. Just as with networking on campus, there is a dramatic increase in value when you can reach *all* of your students, faculty, staff, and other collaborators throughout your region. There is a dramatic increase in value when you can reach every home and every office. This is why so many see the value, and the social need, to attain *universal service*, the state in which everyone is connected and all can participate.

The Role of Regional Networks in the Development of Advanced Networking

In the mid to late 1980s, the network research community created thirteen regional networks that interconnected groups of research universities across the country. These projects advanced the state of technology and demonstrated the value of network applications to the point that other universities found it beneficial to connect, followed shortly thereafter by commercial laboratories and finally educational institutions and corporations of all types. This process spawned today's Internet and one of the fastest-growing new industries in history.

The early adopters of these new Internet technologies had to connect through major research universities or through regional academic networks until the emergence of commercial networking

vendors, called Internet service providers (ISPs). ISPs today connect millions of commercial and individual customers, but they
have focused on low-cost (and relatively low-performance) services
to establish and hold on to market share. Today we find the pattern
repeating itself for advanced networking, with early-adopter
regional networks, research universities, and their industry partners
in the Internet2 project working together to develop and support
technologies and levels of performance that are not yet available
from ISPs. (See Chapter Three for a detailed description of the
Internet2 project.)

The What and Why of GigaPoPs

A gigaPoP (from *giga,* suggesting very large or very fast, and *PoP,*
meaning point of presence for connections) is a geographic locus of
networking facilities that can support very-high-performance network services between customers and providers. Usually housed in
a special equipment room of a university or a regional network
provider, it is where advanced network consumers can come
together to buy services from network providers. GigaPoPs are being
created in many geographic regions and are often managed by educational institutions or their commercial partners.

In addition to providing connections, gigaPoPs can provide
access to unique facilities, services, or information tailored for the
special needs of the education and research customer. GigaPoPs can
also provide cost savings to their educational members by acting
like buying clubs, with members pooling their demand and sharing
access to commercial Internet services.

In many parts of the country the members of state and regional
education networks share in the development of a gigaPoP that
serves all connected members. As with the early Internet, these
regional interconnections of the education community provide new
sets of services for new virtual communities, both inside and outside the original research collaborations.

But gigaPoPs can be much more than just a physical connection point. GigaPoPs are also a human organization, a place where members can share expertise, resources, problems, solutions, and applications. University experts might work with colleagues from federal laboratories and industry, for example, to develop new networking technologies and applications that can be tested on the spot. Scientists from multiple members of the gigaPoP community can collaborate using the larger capacities and advanced services it provides, thereby experiencing the future of networking before it is commercially available.

GigaPoPs also can provide access to professional expertise and services that would not be available to member universities in any other way. They can work together, for example, to train and build campus networking staff by sharing access to other technically savvy engineers. In some regions this may represent the only realistic avenue for ongoing, nearby professional development in such a rapidly emerging field. A campus participating in a gigaPoP is participating in more than the technology—it is participating in a many-faceted community of experts and scholars who share information and tools.

As might be expected, some of the largest gigaPoPs are forming in major metropolitan areas that have especially good access to network service providers. Competition in such areas may drive prices far below those available in more remote locations. Such a metropolitan gigaPoP that is also connected to a regional or state network can serve its members well by connecting them to many potential providers.

If your campus is not already a member of a gigaPoP, how can you find one? The Internet2 Web pages (www.internet2.edu) are a good starting point, or you can try looking at the network map of a large national network that supports education and research, such as the National Science Foundation's vBNS (www.vbns.net/logical.html) or the University Corporation for Advanced Internet

Development's Abilene network (www.internet2.edu/abilene/).
Many national telecommunications carriers interconnect in the
same cities. These hub cities are natural sites for major gigaPoPs,
and the larger universities in these cities are likely points for the
gigaPoPs to grow. The network manager of your nearest major university or regional network is an appropriate person to ask about the
particular situation in your region.

Regional Networks and GigaPoPs as Community Networks

Often regional networks and gigaPoPs are associated with existing
community networks. In this role they may provide both standard
and advanced Internet services to a broader community, including
K–12 schools, public libraries, local government offices, health centers, and even business and industry sites. This, of course, provides
an even broader base for collaboration with members in higher education.

The Role of Regional Networks in Transforming the Educational Community

Once a community has been linked with advanced networking
capabilities, the real work begins. By this I mean the transformation
of campuses and their relationships with their partners to take full
advantage of the new opportunities for collaboration. Campuses
that already share academic or business relationships will have a
head start in streamlining and extending these activities through
the network. Others may need to start from the beginning, developing active relationships as well as networks. Much additional
work on extending relationships can be expected in either case, as
the community adapts to a networked environment.

Early efforts to collaborate in conducting research may begin
with the submission of proposals by e-mail, then move to sharing
daily snapshots of ideas and results with collaborators on private
Web pages, supporting research teams with electronic discussion

lists, and cooperating in drafting new proposals for funding and joint operations that formalize electronic relationships, including those among principal investigators, students, and support staff in organized virtual teams.

Early efforts to collaborate in providing instruction often begin with broadcasting invited speakers and advanced seminars over the Web and helping students at one institution to take rare classes in special subjects offered by another institution over the network. Efforts then move to joint planning of partially shared on-line curricula and even to sharing of academic departments, with faculty hired and coordinated by specialty across the institutions of a consortium to create a "virtual faculty," available to each campus, that is stronger than any individual institution's on-site faculty. Corresponding pressures to share administrative processes such as admissions, articulation, advising, and related financial transactions through the network result in a parallel set of agreements and operational changes in the support organizations of the campuses involved.

Libraries may first implement simply a networked version of their existing interlibrary loan program, but they are soon faced with the need to share on-line content through the network. This leads to a broader discussion of licensing content across institutions, corresponding new business models, and eventually to the possibility of fundamental changes in ownership and control. Although such issues may be easier to address between the campuses of an existing system, they will certainly arise in other natural communities as well.

Conclusion

Advanced networks have the power to transform teaching and learning, scholarship and research, regional and community services, and administration, in both subtle and major ways. Each area will bring its own challenges, many of which will involve changing long-standing policies, practices, business models, and even laws according to the needs and circumstances of the institutions. Some of the most difficult challenges may involve changing established institutional priorities and human habits. All of these challenges can be better met by joining a community of institutions embarked on a similar path.

Working with your neighbors is one of the best ways to get your campus involved with both the development and the use of new technologies, for education as well as research purposes. It is also a good way to get ready for the many important opportunities that will arise later from the commercial Internet.

6

Toward a National Policy to Broaden Academic Participation in Advanced Networking

George O. Strawn, David A. Staudt

The U.S. government, and particularly the National Science Foundation (NSF), played a vital role in the development of the Internet. A series of NSF grant programs extended the original network from a research project linking a few sites to a major communications channel, called the NSFNET, that connected most of higher education. The process of broadening access to the NSFNET to all of higher education resulted in a strong core of technical expertise in this new technology on our campuses, which remains to this day. In addition, it created a large and enthusiastic population of research scientists, educators, students, and others willing to experiment with the new network and develop and share major new applications. The very practice of research was transformed as a result. The early success of the higher education community in computer networking spurred related applications for business and government, resulting in today's booming Internet-related industries.

Any opinions, findings, and conclusions or recommendations expressed in this chapter are those of the authors and do not necessarily reflect the views of the National Science Foundation.

Today the technologies that will enable a dramatically more capable network, the Next Generation Internet (NGI), are under development by a partnership composed of government, industry, and academic researchers (www.ngi.gov). The resulting advanced networks promise to transform access to new forms of education and communication on a global scale. Yet access to the features and capabilities of advanced networking is not presently within reach of most institutions of higher education. It is time once again to consider a national program to broaden access throughout the higher education community.

Such a program would enhance the capability of institutions throughout the nation to participate in research collaborations and would thereby strengthen our national research capability through the inclusion of a wider pool of expertise, talent, and potential. Access to advanced networking throughout higher education would also improve educational opportunities in all communities, improving our chances of developing the technically skilled workforce that we will need in the future.

Extending access today is very different from building the Internet the first time. This time, a vibrant Internet industry is present to supply services to customers. What is needed now is an incentive program that brings together the strengths of our research-focused, already-connected universities, the Internet industry, state governments, and local industry. This group, working in partnership with colleges and universities, could achieve broad participation in advanced networking much sooner, rather than later. The entire nation would reap the benefits.

Why It Is Important to Broaden Participation

Expanding the capability for advanced networking throughout the entire U.S. community of higher education would serve the following three national goals identified in the NSF strategic plan *NSF in a Changing World* (National Science Foundation, 1995):

1. *Enable the United States to uphold a position of world leadership in all aspects of science, mathematics, and engineering.* It is well established that advanced networking will be required even to participate, and certainly to lead the world, in the future activities of science, mathematics, and engineering. (Indeed, this is an underlying theme of this book.) Broadening the reach of advanced networking to include all U.S. higher education institutions would allow maximum possible participation in our national process of discovery and help us find and educate all who can participate in our next century of scientific discovery. Every college that supports research will need to have access to advanced networking to attract and retain research faculty, and advanced network connections will greatly facilitate research collaborations between small or remote campuses and major research centers.

2. *Promote the discovery, integration, dissemination, and employment of new knowledge in service to society.* A partnership that includes our institutions of higher learning, state governments, local industries, and the Internet industry would bring together the right community to rapidly disseminate to society the benefits of advanced networking. The development path of the first Internet traveled from the laboratory to global society by way of such a partnership involving higher education. This same route has much to offer again.

3. *Achieve excellence in U.S. science, mathematics, engineering, and technology education at all levels.* Advanced networking capabilities soon will be required—not just desired—to support the type of on-line, interactive simulations and experiments that will be a hallmark of quality learning materials both on and off campus. Rapid access to databases and digital libraries, including recent discoveries and real-time information, will be required on a daily basis in education for science, engineering, and technology, as well as in research.

We would be well served by a system that supports access to our most modern communications tools for all of our institutions of higher education. Uneven access could greatly limit the opportunities available to large numbers of our scholars and citizens and would ultimately restrict and diminish our national pool of scientific talent. Universal access to advanced networking would make the best tools available to all, advancing the capabilities of individuals and of our nation at the same time.

How to Achieve Broad Participation

It has been well documented that federal leadership can accelerate the development and adoption of revolutionary technologies. This section recalls several examples of past federal leadership and suggests an approach that could serve the present need to accelerate the availability of advanced networking in higher education.

Historical Programs for Development and Adoption

During the 1840s, federal support helped construct the first telegraph link, from Baltimore to Washington, D.C. From 1965 to 1985, federal programs supported research and development in packet-switched data networking and its initial application for research in the ARPANET. From 1985 to 1995, federal programs extended access to a much larger research community in higher education through the NSFNET. And for the past decade, federal support has accelerated the broad use of the Internet in higher education, as NSF helped more than two thousand colleges and universities connect to the Internet. This action stimulated the development of the commercial Internet industry.

Present Programs for Development and Adoption

At present, the federal NGI program supports partnerships between government, industry, and higher education in research and development for high-performance networks. As of the spring of 1999, competitive awards had been made for the establishment of high-performance connections to 150 research universities.

In 1998 and 1999, the President's Information Technology Advisory Committee (PITAC) conducted a review of the NGI program, as Congress required in the NGI authorization legislation. The committee expressed its support for the NGI program and for continued funding for it in a letter to the president dated April 28, 1999 (President's Information Technology Advisory Committee, 1999b). This letter further noted that the overall national investment in research and development for information technology is seriously inadequate. It expressed support for a major additional investment, as recommended in the PITAC report (President's Information Technology Advisory Committee, 1999a), as well as for a corresponding initiative recommended by the president, known as Information Technology for the Twenty-First Century, or IT² (www.ccic.gov/it2/).

In addition, the PITAC review evaluated a criterion called *reach* that measures how far the NGI program has penetrated the broader community of higher education. Their analysis revealed little reach outside the leading research institutions, but as the report points out, the NGI program was not designed or funded to reach the broad higher education community:

> *Reach:* The NGI initiative cannot directly address reach to rural, inner-city, minority, or small institutions. NGI is a research and development program to provide the technologies and applications required as foundations for the next generations of the Internet. It is a relatively small initiative that funds peer-reviewed research proposals. The announced NGI awards cover 150 of the nation's 2,200 four-year, college-level educational institutions. It cannot fund institutions where research is not emphasized and where there is little experience developing advanced networking or applications. The end of

this report makes a specific recommendation to address this issue.

Geographic Reach: While the NGI initiative was not planned or directed to address reach in general, access for otherwise qualified universities with fundable research proposals must not be disadvantaged merely because of their location. NSF expanded the High Performance Connections program to cover all 50 states and has made 33 grants in 18 EPSCoR states. Eventually, NGI research on wireless, hybrid, and satellite technologies may reduce the cost and improve the services available to all users including those in geographically remote areas.

Minority- and Small-College Reach: The NGI was not funded to address Internet access for historically black, Hispanic-serving, Native American, or small colleges and universities. Based on its standard peer review process, NSF has awarded High Performance Connection grants to one historically black and five Hispanic-serving institutions. [President's Information Technology Advisory Committee, 1999b]

The PITAC letter of review closed with several recommendations, including the following specific recommendation on reach:

The Committee shares Congress' concern that no Federal program addresses the reach issue. We recommend Congress consider additional funding for a program where the NGI research institutions act as aggregators and mentors for nearby smaller or disadvantaged institutions. This is primarily infrastructure, not networking research and, hence, not part of the proposed IT^2 program. [President's Information Technology Advisory Committee, 1999b]

Recommendation for a Future Program
to Broaden Participation

It is not feasible for the federal government to single-handedly fund the extension of advanced networking to every college and university in the nation. Moreover, such a comprehensive model was not even used for the original Internet; the NSF Connections to the Internet program leveraged private and campus funds many times greater than the amount of the federal awards and required full support by the campus (in each case) after only two years of partial federal support.

What is feasible and necessary today is a redesigned incentive program that again greatly leverages federal investment and achieves lasting results. This can best be accomplished through partnerships that are chosen to reflect the local circumstances of each institution. Partnerships should bring together the following critical players in a design that can be tailored to best fit the individual situation.

- *Candidate colleges or universities.* Candidate institutions would need to provide a written plan and demonstrate the ability and commitment to engage in technical and financial cooperation with the other partners sufficient to lead from initial development to permanent, stable access and operations.

- *Already-connected research universities (in all fifty states).* These institutions would provide regional access to key technical leadership for advanced networking. They are potential points for aggregation and operation of regional advanced networks and potential partners in research and education applications.

- *Local industry.* Local firms would function as partners in funding and sharing regional facilities and partners in workforce and economic development.

- *State governments.* State governments would function
  as major partners in funding initiatives for advanced
  networking for higher education and possibly as partners in construction and operations.

- *Federal government.* As noted previously, the federal
  government was the original funder of research and
  development for the Internet; it is the present funder of
  research and development for high-performance networking; and it would play a leadership role in creating
  partnerships through participating research universities. Figure 6.1 illustrates the possible relationships
  between these potential partners.

As a whole, this partnership arrangement resembles aspects of
the U.S. Innovation Partnerships, initially described by the U.S.
Department of Commerce in a press release dated February 3, 1997.
In that press release, Commerce Under Secretary for Technology
Dr. Mary L. Good stated, "By working together, the states and Federal R&D agencies can strengthen our national innovation system.
Innovation drives economic growth and raises living standards and
each of the partners to this new effort brings unique strengths and
perspectives. Federal R&D focuses on basic research, Federal missions, and developing emerging and enabling technologies; states
often work directly with companies to bring knowledge into the
commercial marketplace. Working together, we can maximize the
impact of science and technology on jobs, economic growth, and
living standards." The press release went on to describe how the
partnership would work:

Under the new partnership, the White House and Federal agencies will work with states on such issues as:

- Removing regulatory barriers to the adoption of new
  technologies in such areas as telemedicine, environ-

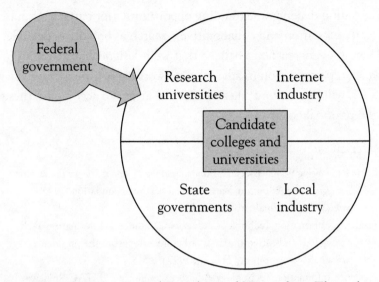

Figure 6.1. Partners Extending Advanced Networking Throughout Higher Education

mental technologies, and the building and construction industries;

- Developing programs to stimulate technology investments in rural and other states that traditionally receive less Federal research funding;

- Addressing the technical, legal, and other issues associated with the expansion of electronic commerce.

Conclusion

Higher education has played a central role in the development of both today's Internet and advanced networking. Advanced networking will play a critical role throughout higher education. We as a nation depend on extending opportunities for participation in quality education and collaborative research as broadly as possible. There is every reason to believe that well-designed partnerships to broaden participation in advanced networking to all of higher education will be an affordable and effective means to accomplish these vital national goals.

References

NSF in a Changing World. Executive Summary of the National Science Foundation's Strategic Plan. Arlington, Va.: National Science Foundation, 1995. [www.nsf.gov.od/lpa/strtplan/strtplan.pdf]

President's Information Technology Advisory Committee. "Information Technology Research: Investing in Our Future." Report to the president. [www.ccic.gov/ac/report]. Feb. 24, 1999a.

President's Information Technology Advisory Committee. "PITAC Review of the Next Generation Internet Program and Related Issues." [www.ccic.gov/ac/pitac_ngi_review.html]. Apr. 28, 1999b.

U.S. Department of Commerce. "White House and Governors Announce Technology Partnership, Commerce Department Will Play Lead Role." Press release. [www.ta.doc.gov/PRel/pr2397.htm]. Feb. 3, 1997.

Finding the Will and the Way

Ellen Earle Chaffee

The annual lists of the nation's one hundred "most wired" campuses from *Yahoo Internet Life* magazine are incomplete. The magazine's first college survey went to a few hundred institutions selected on the basis of expert judgment. Many institutions complained about being left out of the survey sample. The planners then expanded and formalized the sampling procedure to include very large campuses, selective-admissions campuses, and high-level technical and engineering universities, as well as those that had made it onto previous most-wired lists. They may have expected that these criteria would encompass all campuses with the most advanced uses of computer technologies in the nation. After all, high technology is expensive and requires highly skilled faculty and staff, so it is reasonable to expect more of it at large, wealthy, prestigious institutions.

Two small public baccalaureate-degree-granting institutions in North Dakota that emphasize teacher education and business did not make *Yahoo Internet Life*'s survey list, either in the first year or in subsequent years after the criteria were expanded. This is unfortunate, but understandable. North Dakota's state funding per student consistently ranks among the bottom five in the nation, as do its faculty salary levels. Tuition for the 750 to 1,100 students at these two campuses is about $2,000 per year. These schools are in small communities in a rural state with minimal access to advanced networking capabilities. They cannot place orders large enough to attract sponsorships or secure major discounts from technology firms. Yet their responses to the 1999 *Yahoo Internet Life* survey, submitted through the back door and rejected by the magazine, suggest that they would be near the top of the list. Every student and faculty member has access twenty-four hours per day, seven days a week, in classrooms, offices, residence halls, and off-campus locations, to a high-powered notebook computer, nearly all of the peripherals assessed by the survey, and the Internet. Each campus has 1,200 laptop ports. The universities spend the equivalent of over 10 percent of their annual budgets on hardware and software every year. The only student services not available over the Web are those controlled at the state level.

Most people observing technology in higher education have never heard of these two institutions. Few would expect campuses like these to make extensive use of technology.

Taking the Lead

Valley City State University (VCSU) and Mayville State University (MSU) provide all faculty and students with notebook computers. VCSU started this practice in 1996 and MSU in 1997—the second and fourth institutions in the nation to adopt this approach. Nearly all classrooms include power and network connections at every student seat, with multimedia presentation equipment in each room. Networked printers are scattered throughout the campuses, along with convenient access to scanners, digital still and video cameras, CD-ROM burners, and other digital tools. The libraries provide access to a wealth of digital resources, both on campus and via the Internet. Students have ample storage space for e-mail and Web pages.

An illustrative case study in "Technology and the New Professional Teacher: Preparing for the 21st Century" (Task Force on

Technology and Teacher Education, 1997) describes the typical student experience in teacher education at VCSU (which is comparable to that at MSU):

> Before going to class I access my e-mail to read responses from two instructors regarding clarification of assignments, four messages from fellow students, and a message from my mom who lives on the opposite side of the state. I make revisions for my part of our cooperative learning group's PowerPoint presentation for a class later in the week.
>
> I use my laptop in my first class to take notes from the PowerPoint presentation the professor is giving. I'm creating a Web page for this class and later this week I'll videotape myself teaching a mathematics lesson. Then I'll digitize the video clip and link it to my mathematics Web page.
>
> I'm working on a portfolio project in my language arts class, and the other students and I are in the process of scanning pictures into our PowerPoint presentations. We have all had the opportunity to develop electronic portfolios this semester and we are getting ready to complete them so that we can turn them into a CD-ROM. We will present our portfolio projects to the rest of the class during finals week. Each of us has been compiling digitized video of lessons taught, various scanned pictures, and other pertinent information that will help us to demonstrate what we have learned in the class this past semester. [www.ncate.org/projects/tech/ci6.html]

The network is essential to gaining this instructional impact from technology. Some faculty rely on Web-based resources instead of textbooks. Web-based courses are commonplace and, along with e-mail capabilities, greatly enhance student understanding of course structure and content. One day early in the first semester of computer use, the server crashed for three hours on a Monday morning. When restored, the cache of e-mail messages averaged fifteen per student and faculty member.

The universities have created chief information officer (CIO) positions to support the initiative. The CIOs report to the academic vice president, confirming that the primary purpose of universal computing is to improve learning. They have expanded their help desk staff, predominantly with student workers. Each campus has a representative committee to provide strategic advice and set budget priorities for technology.

The communities that host the universities have recognized the initiative as a strategic asset for their economic development efforts. Each is working with its local campus to establish a regional technology center to support significant expansions in information technology businesses.

The institutional cultures at these universities are changing as a result of the initiative. Faculty members accept advice and help from students more readily. They change their course materials and teaching methods more often. They routinely enroll in on-campus workshops, often taught by their colleagues, to build skills. Student self-confidence is rising, as they have begun to understand the value of their information technology skills both for learning and for work.

The total cumulative cost of the notebook initiative on each campus over the last three years is nearly equal to the entire annual operating budget of the campus. The current annual cost of the initiative is equal to about 10 percent of each institution's annual operating budget. Yet the universities have received no state funding for this project. Grants, student fees, and reallocation are the only revenue sources.

So why have so few people heard about Mayville State and Valley City State? They are beginning to appear in a few national publications—primarily publications by professional associations and scholars, plus the *New York Times*. But for the most part, these schools are invisible. They are too small and disconnected to gain attention or concessions from vendors. They are too remote for the national higher education press. Oddly enough, being on the frontier of change makes it difficult to gain attention. Just as it was hard for people to imagine how different life would be if everyone had telephones or fax machines, they cannot appreciate the transformative changes that occur with universal computing. The practical value of the first fax machine was nil. The more fax machines that went into operation, however, the more valuable each became. The changes with universal computing are both concrete and ineffable, both immediate and long-term. And they are difficult to comprehend until you experience them.

Benefits and Challenges

In addition to the instructional benefits to faculty and students that the notebook initiative has provided, MSU and VCSU are finding institutional advantages from the initiative as well. In a state with declining numbers of high school graduates, both institutions experienced over 20 percent increases in freshmen enrollments in fall 1998. This, despite the fact that the computer fee increased the tuition and fees bill by nearly 50 percent. It appears that word of mouth can compensate for lack of marketing funds.

The computer fee enables the universities to capitalize on the latest advances in technology, replacing an equipment replacement cycle of ten-plus years under state funding with a two-year cycle. The increase in computing support costs is modest because of standardized software and hardware, with users left on their own to find support for any additional software they prefer. Initially controversial, software standardization is now accepted as an advantage for communication.

One of the more subtle but powerful effects of universal computing is like that of the Internet itself—it is inherently democratic.

All students and faculty, regardless of their means, are gaining knowledge and skills that could well be assets that make a critical difference in their lives.

Faculty can use resources and teaching methods that would otherwise be impractical to use or unavailable to them, yet they have not ceded the right to teach in traditional fashion. Those who are eager for change have that option. Those who prefer not to change experience pressures only if students are dissatisfied. Universal computing has been a powerful revitalizing force for the faculty.

The next development on both campuses is customized learning—making the curriculum increasingly available on an anytime, anywhere, any pace basis. Recognizing that other institutions have deep pockets for developing distance education curricula, the focus is on breaking the time barriers on a traditional campus, with greater attention to student outcomes and less to seat time or schedules. These changes will better accommodate student learning styles, backgrounds, and goals. They will better mesh with work schedules for learners of any age. Therefore, they will enable the universities to seek new markets, to adjust for the decline in traditional markets.

The universities are also using technology to forge partnerships with business and international institutions. They send exchange students to Mexico for student teaching, maintaining close contact by e-mail. They have developed a customized curriculum to meet the entry-level knowledge and skill requirements of a major software firm in the region. These and other partnerships have expanded the horizons and opportunities of both students and faculty in this isolated area.

Universal computing provides opportunities for increased efficiency and communication. For example, we prepared testimony for both universities' legislative budget hearings entirely by e-mail, from soliciting participation by eight guest speakers in five different locations to making their travel arrangements and helping them prepare their presentations. When university officials attend key meetings, they often write summary notes and send them by e-mail to colleagues that very day. In the past, important news might have waited several days or weeks until the next scheduled meeting. And it is just as easy, at no additional cost, to send notes to twenty people as to two. Secretaries are left freer to perform more important tasks; rather than typing and printing correspondence for others, they may well be setting up meetings or handling more correspondence for their supervisors on their own. The clutter of paper-stuffed campus mailboxes is gone. In addition, campuswide e-mail has proven invaluable for rapid response in times of crisis, such as when rumors of food poisoning surfaced and when four students died in an auto accident.

The notebook initiative has also brought special challenges to the universities. Chief among them is dealing with the shortage of information technology personnel, both faculty and staff, and the extraordinary market pressures on their salaries. People in small rural teaching institutions tend to expect salary equity, regardless of discipline. The administration recently concluded that it must offer up to 50 percent more than what would otherwise be considered equitable to attract and retain key information technology personnel. Special efforts are under way to assist campus people in other fields who are interested in becoming qualified for the higher-paying positions. The budget impact could become overwhelming, given the already tight financial situation.

The universities are no longer in a position to ignore or defer investments to keep pace with rapid changes in technology. At this point, completing a high-speed telecommunications infrastructure is the major challenge, due to the cost of bringing this capability to rural areas. The initial expectation that computers could be replaced on a three-year cycle has yielded to the understanding that two years is the limit because the machines are too outdated in the third year.

New faculty members are rarely as knowledgeable regarding information technology tools and skills as those who helped launch the initiative. Even long-term faculty members require continual professional development to stay abreast of new options. The universities have, in effect, no budget for faculty professional development, yet somehow they have addressed the most critical needs to date.

Lessons for Leaders

Most institutions are struggling to define and meet technology-related goals, and different solutions will be appropriate for different campuses. These two universities have found a solution that is working for them now, although continued change is inevitable. Their experience to date suggests some lessons that should inform their own ongoing change and may be useful to others as well.

The decision to pursue universal computing was a vital factor in positioning the universities for a viable future, providing them with a new market and a unique niche for the region. Nevertheless, the preliminary discussions about making the change focused heavily on the anticipated benefits to students and learning, and this focus remains central. Despite the strong emphasis on the notebook initiative, technology is firmly treated as a means, not an end. This suggests two lessons: *one effective way to meet external challenges is to create corresponding internal challenges,* and *it's important to keep your eyes on the right target.*

We are entering a new era for higher education, as numerous articles and books portend. The challenges may be greater than ever before, requiring unprecedented change in many institutions. To meet the challenge of universal computing, these universities developed skills, knowledge, and attitudes that will serve them well in a fast-paced future. Institutional personnel visit campuses and businesses, employ a cohort model of mutual support, use a formal peer mentoring process, and share information among themselves informally. The universities targeted discretionary funds for individuals and invested in early adopters. They reexamined and revised their incentive and reward systems, including their faculty evaluation process. They had a great advantage in that nearby University of

Minnesota–Crookston was the national pioneer in institution-provided universal computing. Many people there were exceptionally generous in sharing their ideas and experience, with sometimes alarming candor. Faculty, staff, and student visits to Crookston and other innovative campuses in the region were a critical factor in gaining acceptance of the change and examples of how (and how not) to do it. University personnel became increasingly committed to the change, building their capacity to meet and surmount "impossible" barriers. This was especially fortunate since new barriers arose as old ones disappeared. This suggests a third lesson: *people don't resist change—they resist being changed; therefore, use multiple high-involvement strategies to build interest and capacity for change.*

With specific reference to technology-based change, the institutions also learned these lessons:

- *The top priority is supportive faculty development, before launch and ever after.* "I have spent sixteen years making myself the best teacher I know how to be. Please, please, don't put me in a position that undermines everything I've been working for. Don't make me look stupid," said one faculty member. Not only do faculty deserve institutional support in maintaining their professional integrity, but also the quality of teaching and learning will decrease if they must adopt new methods without adequate preparation.

- *Staff need professional development, too.* For a while, the requirements of a particular grant did not allow staff to attend some professional development sessions. Their morale plummeted. They have professional pride, too, and many became highly enthusiastic leaders in using technology.

- *Using technology can achieve both academic and administrative efficiencies, but don't expect it to cost less or reduce workloads.* Secretaries feared for their jobs when word processing began to take hold, but appetites for more work, faster output, and higher-quality results increased more rapidly than did affordable technology. In other words, the better the work that was produced, the more work was demanded. These universities expected, or at least hoped, that savings from dropping inefficient old ways of doing business would eventually offset the costs of new ways. It doesn't work that way.

- *Using technology presents major challenges of reinventing almost everything you do.* As a result of instituting universal computing, these universities have begun to question their definition of an academic course, the accepted qualifications for faculty, the content and organization of faculty work, the relative value of staff versus faculty, the criteria for faculty evaluation, their course registration systems, their methods of charging for services, and their methods of counting enrollments . . . among other things.

- *Small size is an advantage for technological innovation; rural location is a disadvantage.* Rapid, widespread change comes easier to a smaller, highly interactive, relatively homogeneous institution than to a large, diverse one. Differences of opinion are fewer, needs are more similar, and informal interactions can substantially aid the change process. However, technological innovations that depend on installing a high-end telecommunications infrastructure may be difficult in rural areas due to cost. Federal government support such as was provided for rural electrification may be required.

- *If you pursue universal computing, don't forget staff—all staff.* Secretaries want notebook computers so they can take work home. Highly mobile physical plant personnel worry that they are missing important campus announcements when they must rely on someone else to print e-mail messages for them.

- *Standardization is your friend.* Computing support personnel may be the primary beneficiaries of standardization, but users benefit, too. For years, my secretaries on each campus used different word processing software, and then they had two different versions of the same one. Finally, we need no longer make translations for each other. Now that everyone is using the same software, people can get help from almost anyone nearby, rather than having to contact the help desk. The transition to standardization may be rocky for some, but the benefits include both reduced support needs and easier communication.

- *Increased cost is not a barrier to enrollment, and it may even be an asset, if the value added is obvious.* North Dakotans are exceptionally price-sensitive. Some community members thought the universities were committing enrollment suicide when they added the hefty computer fee. Instead, enrollment is stable or increasing, with no apparent cost effect. As news spreads that graduates are obtaining high-salary jobs of their choice because of their technology skills, the value received will become even more apparent.

- *Students can be powerful allies for institutional change.* Conscious of paying "extra" for the computers, students are becoming increasingly sophisticated educational consumers. They expect heavy use of technology, but not for its own sake. When "the old way" is better, they insist on using it. In short, students are teaching the faculty, through their responses, how to use technology effectively.

Conclusion

Mayville State University and Valley City State University are demonstrating that technology-enriched instruction can be both educationally sound and strategically advantageous. Students are becoming savvy not only about technology and the curriculum but also, through the Internet, about the world beyond their state's borders. Communication and relationships between faculty, students, and staff are stronger. Collaboration with business and the community is expanding. But perhaps most amazing, all this is happening at no additional cost to the state, which provides relatively little even for traditional instruction. It can be done. And it is well worth doing.

Reference

Task Force on Technology and Teacher Education, National Council for Accreditation of Teacher Education. "Technology and the New Professional Teacher: Preparing for the 21st Century." [www.ncate.org/projects/tech/TECH.HTM]. 1997.

What Campus Leaders Can Do Today

Mark A. Luker

The nine contributing authors of this book have explored the impact of advanced networking on higher education from a variety of perspectives. Together, we tell a compelling story of what this technology will mean and how we must actively prepare for the opportunities and challenges it presents.

What Have We Learned?

We have learned that the Internet has already had a profound effect on higher education. Indeed, it has already transformed research by allowing remote access to instruments and instant communications; it has transformed our access to information by enabling rapid and inexpensive publication on the Web; and it has transformed human communications by supporting the creation of virtual collaborative groups.

The Internet is beginning to transform education itself, but it has had less impact in higher education than in other areas of society, for three principal reasons:

- Off-campus access to an advanced network remains poor, very expensive, or even nonexistent in many regions of the world.

- Performance limitations of the Internet inhibit the full use of rich multimedia content and communications.

- Learningware development remains in the early-adopter phase.

Yet we know that many parties are working toward an advanced Internet that will solve these problems by supporting high-quality, natural communications with voice and video and providing rapid, reliable access anywhere and anytime. And all this will come at an affordable price, due to the emergence of commercial Internet services that support the convergence of all types of electronic communications.

We know that information technology (IT) will be able to support high-quality, active learning experiences that match a wider variety of learner styles and needs than does conventional instruction and that the advanced Internet will make these experiences available to students anywhere, anytime. These developments are coming just in time to meet the anticipated tremendous increase in demand for quality education in the global knowledge society. Networked campuses are revolutionary in that they will change the basic roles of students and faculty, the business models of higher education, and higher education's basic organizational structures; consequently, advanced networking will face formidable cultural and policy barriers within institutions of higher education, and these barriers will need to be addressed.

We have learned that the advanced Internet will transform our libraries, providing access for distant students and scholars as well as new content and services on campus. The advanced Internet, along with evolving forms of live access to changing information, will change even the very concepts of publication. But just as it will in higher education as a whole, advanced networking will change the basic roles of patrons and librarians, the business models of libraries and publishers, and traditional organizational structures in academic libraries, and consequently it will encounter cultural and policy barriers that will need to be addressed.

We have learned that the technologies for an advanced Internet are now being actively studied for use in higher education, by a three-way partnership between government, industry, and academia known as the Internet2 project. This and related projects at individual campuses and regional networks often require the coordination of technical choices and standards across institutional boundaries, and thus they concern a level of leadership well above campus technology faculty and staff. One goal is to develop new applications that can show how the tools and features of the advanced network will work once the network is complete. This is a crucial step, both in inventing the future and in building a broader community of understanding and support for the needed investments and changes. Internet2 is a specialized research and development project involving a small number of research universities; however, the advances it brings will be incorporated into the commercial Internet through competitive innovation, transforming it into an advanced network available to all. In the meantime, organizations such as EDUCAUSE are working to help the broader community of higher education to begin their preparations for that network.

We have also learned that campus leaders must begin today to develop an advanced network on their campus. Fortunately, the technology for such a network is well understood and comes in standard building blocks that can be applied in different ways to meet the needs of different campuses. It is also fortunate that these standard approaches support a gradual evolution of campus networks to meet new demands while still maintaining the right level of service for present needs. Although the costs per user of campus networks is falling rapidly, overall costs for a typical campus will continue to rise substantially for a number of years as the campus network evolves into a full-strength, reliable communications corridor for virtually all institutional activities. Each campus must find and adopt a strategy to secure regular, ongoing funding for the development and renewal of its network. One of the most difficult challenges today is to find or develop—and then keep—a staff with the requisite leadership, customer service, and technology skills.

Many campuses find that a very good way to get started and to maintain momentum in advanced networking is to work collaboratively with similar or nearby institutions. Such collaborations may reduce the costs of networking, by allowing institutions to share certain circuits and services. More important, they can provide a shared source of professional development and technical support, supplying critical new skills and technologies that are not readily available on the market. Ideally, such collaborations will coincide with existing institutional ties that support the institutions' missions. Creating technical partnerships between institutions is also a good way to promote and support academic collaborations, such as shared digital libraries and shared academic programs made available over the campus networks, a clear win for all.

We have learned that the success of the present Internet has led to numerous calls for the federal government to "do it again" by promoting the spread of advanced networking throughout the academic community. Although today's environment of commercial networking is entirely different from the environment when the NSFNET was first built, many believe that the federal government should play a role in stimulating investments by states and communities to provide access to advanced networking at every site of higher education. Such access is needed to maintain our present national lead in the networking and IT industries. More important, it will strengthen our entire system of education to better support the emerging knowledge society.

Finally, we have learned that campus leaders need not wait to achieve great success in networking. Much is possible with today's Internet, and without investing a lot of new dollars, as much depends on changing the things we do and the ways we do them.

Strong, optimistic, consensus leadership at the highest levels is critical for such institutional transformations.

What Can Campus Leaders Do Today?

Although advanced networking, and especially its application to higher education, is just now emerging into the mainstream, it is critical that campus leaders prepare their institutions today for the changes ahead. What can and should be done now?

- *Develop a shared campus vision.* Perhaps most important is to develop a shared campus vision concerning the value and future impact of advanced networking on the institution. It is critical for campus opinion leaders, decision makers, and other important stakeholders to understand and agree that a transformation is important and that it must be a central matter of campus planning and strategy. These stakeholders must see the power of what will soon be available—not just the limitations of what we can do today. This can be arranged through selected critical demonstrations, field trips to other sites, and exposure at national meetings to sites and projects that are well ahead of the present average. The Internet is famous for moving the leading edge today to the commonly available tomorrow at rates measured in months, not years.

- *Build consensus through a campuswide strategic plan.* It is crucial to define a vision and craft a written strategic plan for networking and IT on campus that are understood and embraced far beyond the technical faculty and staff. All key stakeholders must see the Internet (including the campus network) as the fundamental platform on which all information and communication-based resources and services will be deployed. This is a matter of campus culture, not just technology. The new culture thrives on the acceptance of compatible standards rather than the proliferation of special exceptions. It achieves affordability by adopting commodity or off-the-shelf products rather than build-it-yourself experiments. Success depends on getting absolutely everyone connected, not just most people. Once an institution is successfully providing all possible service functions over the campus network, it can offer the same functions at a distance, and at almost no marginal cost. Institutional leaders must nurture this consensus and build on it to permanently reallocate funding and human resources and to energize the corresponding requirements of institutional and human change.

- *Establish an effective, integrated IT organization.* As more and more of its critical services are moved to its network and become dependent on it, a campus must create an effective organization that addresses all aspects of human and technical support for IT. It will no longer be effective to operate separate organizations based on traditional technologies such as telephones, television, or data networking. It will not make sense to separate the support for one kind of computing from the support for another or to operate multiple organizations to provide help on different services.

- *Articulate a base level of IT services.* The campus IT organization must work with the campus community to define a base-level collection of IT services that will be supported at high quality for all. Successfully defining this base-level functionality is a critical and ongoing exercise in consensus building. Providing adequate support for the base level of services will often require dropping other services or supporting them out of special budgets for special reasons. Long-term institutional success will certainly require abandoning "not-invented-here" attitudes and full consideration of outsourcing where appropriate. Perhaps most important, it will require that the campus get serious and get organized to meet the demands of good customer service.

- *Identify network leadership and funding at the campus level.* Each institution must secure high-level, big-picture leadership for planning its network on an ongoing basis. It must move this part of the business out of the realm of grants, crises, and one-time special events to an ongoing part of the budget, creating a secure and regular source of funding for a robust and evolving campus network. It must build all future services on the network. These are issues for top leadership—they are not likely to bubble up to become top campus priorities from within an existing IT organization.

- *Build partnerships and foster interinstitutional collaboration.* Campus leaders must take the initiative in establishing and promoting institutional collaborations at the community, regional, and national level for the implementation of network-based applications in education, research, or services. These are no longer issues of technology but are questions of basic mission and approach. A campus can join or even form a regional network, it can actively participate in relevant national organizations, and it can involve an ever-wider circle of its opinion leaders in developing a shared vision of networking for higher education.

- *Provide strong leadership for change.* Campus leaders must provide the strong personal leadership required to change institutional missions and roles. Transforming a campus takes strong consensus. This is restructuring, not just adding or tweaking. It will require all the skills of leading and managing human and institutional change. Leaders today can rely on tested methods for strategic planning that lead to real change on a reasonable schedule, tested methods for generating the support and buy-in of those who must help, and influential public relations campaigns, both within and outside the community. Leaders will need to lead! In the end, the most critical role for presidents will be the ongoing, personal leadership required for significant institutional change.

Conclusion

The challenges are great—they involve substantial ongoing financial investments, uncertainty surrounding timing and outcomes, the resistance of entrenched structures and procedures, and the normal but limiting barriers to human change. Yet the opportunities are great as well—higher education has the possibility, for the first time, of dramatically improving access to quality education. Other, newer institutions are moving rapidly down the path. It is up to campus leaders to determine how new networking technologies and strategies can best be used to help their specific institutions thrive.

Index

instructional, 62–63, 69; large-
scale, 64–65; networked communities and, 60–70; rationale for, 59,
64–65, 72; regional network,
65–69; research, 60–61, 68–69; university library, 62. *See also* Communities, networked; Partnerships;
Regional networks
Collaboratories, 16, 23, 26
Committee for Inter-institutional
Cooperation (CIC), 61–62
Commodity goods principle, 44;
applied to network electronics, 54,
55
Communities, networked, 59, 60–67;
atmospheric sciences, 61; gigaPoPs
as, 68; institutional, 61–62; instructional, 62–63, 69; large collaborations for, 64–65; multiplier effect
in, 60, 63–64; physics, 60–61;
regional networks as, 68; research,
60–61, 68–69; university, 62
Connection points. *See* GigaPoPs
Consensus building, through campuswide strategic plan, 97–98
Consortia: for bulk licensing agreements, 20, 21, 69; regional networking, 34, 65–69. *See also*
Collaboration; Partnerships
Consortia collaborators, as education
providers, 12
Consumer institutions, as education
providers, 12
Content-searching facilities, 39
Continuous renewal principle, 41–42,
43–44, 47; applied to network elec-
tronics, 54; applied to network pro-
tocols, 55; applied to pathway, 52
Contract law, 20
Convergence, 6, 37–40
Conversion from print to digital,
18–19
Copyright law, 20, 26, 27
Core courses, future pricing of, 12
Costs: of campus networks, 42, 43, 44,
45, 49, 52, 95; collaboration for

containment of, 59, 65; of digitizing
libraries, 19–23, 27; factors in, 5;
good design and, 43; operating versus capital, 43; pathway, 52; of
qualified network staff, 55–56, 87;
of staff training, 51; of universal
notebook computer initiatives in
small institutions, 84, 85, 89–91;
value-based investment principle
and, 44, 49, 54. *See also* Investment
Course communities, networked,
62–63
Course materials, electronic, 25, 84
Cultural issues, 7
Customized learning, 86

D

Databases, electronic, 16, 17
Democracy, universal access and,
85–86
Dictionaries, 17
Digital libraries, 4, 15–28, 94–95;
budget and pricing issues of, 19–23,
27; capital funding for, 22–23, 27;
challenges of, 4; collaboration of,
69; content and roles for, 23–26;
current commercial, 16; current
research, 15–16; defined, 15; organizations for, 4; origins of, 16–17;
physical space needs for, 23; of
scholarly societies, 16, 17; University of California example of, 62;
vision of, 15; World Wide Web as,
15. *See also* Academic libraries
Digital Library Federation, 4
Digital Millennium Copyright Act,
26
Digital production and content services, 39–40
Distance learning: advanced networks
for, 3–4, 8–9, 24, 25, 65; barriers to,
11; college course communities
and, 63; current technology for,
2–3; for graduate classes, 24; multicasting and, 64–65; multimedia
for, 25